AF480859

First Edition 2023, published with Oregon Greystone Press.

This book is a work of nonfiction.

Printed in the United States of America

ISBN 979-8-218-21813-3

Cover design and interior design by Chris Miller Design.

"Silence is not golden, it is covered in blood."
—Don DuPay

"Poverty is the parent of revolution and *crime."*
—Aristotle

Praise

Like fellow scribe Raymond Chandler, Don DuPay aims straight ahead in black and white. The color comes from a descriptive word here, a piece of dialogue there. As a Portland street cop, homicide and burglary detective, he's heard and seen "many people…probably up to no good" – murderers, pimps, hookers, burglars, heroin dealers, and lazy cops. He's fallen in love with a whore. DuPay's reportage stuns the reader and offers no time for rest or sentimentality.

Stylistic crime writers such as Dashiell Hammett, Maj Sjowall, Robert Parker, to name a few, have their favorite locations. Don Dupay has his – Portland, Oregon. He's walked the streets, made the busts, seen dead bodies, listened to liars, and heard every story. Don DuPay invites the reader to ride shotgun with him — laugh, cry, and shake one's head in amazement.

DuPay is at the top of his game as he recounts everything honorable and corrupt about society. After seventeen years as a street cop, homicide, and burglary detective, DuPay traded his badge and .38 revolver for a keyboard. His words are like a song the reader can't get out of his or her head.

Like watching a "Cops" marathon, *The Tainted Rose: Stories from a Portland Detective* is a relentless ride along with one law enforcer. Take a deep breath, pour two fingers of a fine single malt and start reading – you're going to be up all night.

~Robert Crane, co-author of Crane: *Sex, Celebrity, and My Father's Unsolved Murder*

Disillusioned homicide detective Don DuPay has seen and done it all. But when he falls in love with a beautiful black hooker named Artent Thomas this book simply takes off into uncharted territory for true-crime, non-fiction. You'll be as blown away as I was.

~Phil Stanford, author of *Portland Confidential*

DuPay's stories from his days as a cop offer an unflinching, first-person perspective of Portland's shadowy underbelly. Spanning the '60s and '70s, with the perspective of hindsight, history, and humanity, *The Tainted Rose: Stories from a Portland Detective* is a page-turning literary ride-along, told in the hard-boiled noir style of Chandler and Hammett.

-Suzy Vitello, author of *Bitterroot,* 2024

Once again it's Don Dupay's remarkable voice! The voice of an experienced cop, relying on his "cop radar" and street smarts to navigate tough characters, horrific situations, and his own raw emotions. Go with him through these pages of his experience. The stories are deeply personal ones from an extraordinary life, after which Dupay is sadder and wiser. You'll be sadder and wiser for reading his stories. A great companion to *Behind the Badge in River City.*

—Jeff Stookey, author of *Medicine for the Blues trilogy: Acquaintance,* book 1; *Chicago Blues,* book 2; and *Dangerous Medicine,* book 3.

Don DuPay is a keen observer of the behavior and motives of both the police and the criminals they pursue. DuPay's book, TheTainted Rose: Stories From a Portland Detective is a raw, vivid and courageous description of what life was like on the streets of Portland in the 1960s and 1970s. Don was a tough cop and a compassionate one. He tells the stories about how the lives of the police and those who commit crimes become intertwined. DuPay does not mince words about his own transgressions; his stories are awash with humanity and caring while trying to keep the streets safe.

-Mike Lindberg , former Portland City Commissioner

ACKNOWLEDGEMENTS

I would like to thank my good friend Phil Stanford, author of Rose City Vice: Dirty Cops and Dirty Robbers, and Portland Confidential: Sex, Crime and Corruption in the Rose City, for encouraging me to tell the truth about my experiences as a street cop, and later when I worked as a burglary and homicide detective. I thank Phil for sharing his insights into how to flesh out stories and make them unique and for his continued friendship and support over the years.

I would like to thank my wife Theresa's cousins, Mary Lewis and her lovely daughter Elina Lewis for helping with the title for the book. When we asked family and friends to suggest a title of the book, over social media, Mary and Elina came up with the title The Tainted Rose, and my wife and I realized that was indeed the perfect name, so thank you Mary and Elina!

I would like to thank our friend, the late JD Chandler for his friendship, and encouragement in my writing, telling me to "write longer" and to provide more descriptive details. I learned a lot from JD and will never forget his charismatic personality, and how he always remained true to his convictions.

I would like to thank my friend "Katherine," for her friendship and insight into the heroin business in the Albina ghetto during the 1960s and 1970s and for everything she told meback when I was a young cop and later when we were friends in our forties, long after my career with PPB was over and we were both no longer young. Katherine is someone I will never forget.

I would like to thank Jeff Stookey for his wonderful blurb. Jeff has been a supportive and encouraging writer friend who has always provided the most excellent feedback and insight into the writing process and what I should think about doing. Thank you Jeff for your support and friendship!

I would also like to thank Suzy Vitello, Portland author and writing coach, for her wonderful support over the years and for the perfect blurb she wrote in support of this book. Thank you Suzy, it is an honor to know you approve of my work.

Lastly, I would like to thank my wife, writer and author, Theresa Griffin Kennedy, for encouraging me to write my stories as only I can, and for tirelessly performing the duties of a fine and dedicated editor, collaborator and muse.

Table of Contents

North Precinct in St. Johns, illustration by
Truxton Meadows.

The Tainted Rose

Stories From a Portland Detective

By Don DuPay

Oregon Greystone Press
First Edition 2023

Chapter 1
Jewel Thieves: The Daring and the Dumb

"That's the trouble with cops. You're all set to hate their guts and then you meet one that goes human on you."

— Raymond Chandler, *The Long Goodbye*

Prologue: The Portland Zoo, 1969.

The vehicle must have moved slowly up the back service road headed toward the zoo. It was necessary to proceed cautiously in the dark of night without the headlights on so the zoo's cage cleaner, who also served as a Night Watchman of sorts, would not be alerted.

A flashlight held out the window of the vehicle would serve to illuminate the edge of the narrow asphalt road, casting a weak yellow light. The vehicle was probably a truck what with all the equipment it would need to haul: cutting torches, hoses, and an oxygen and acetylene tank, a large roll of thick black plastic to cover the windows of the zoo office, an assortment of chisels and mallets for cutting into the metal of the safe, a heavy industrial drill, and a power cord for drilling into the body of the safe. Lastly, there would be several rolls of Scotch tape used to seal the cracks around the safe door, which never seemed smart to me because Scotch tape was cheap and not very effective.

On that summer night, the vehicle must have slowed to a stop as it came close to the heavy chain hanging across the road halting its access into the zoo. The driver put the vehicle in park and exited the driver's side as quietly as he could. There was an old rusty padlock securing the chain that would have to be dealt with. The driver removed a homemade key from his trouser pocket and unlocked the padlock, allowing the chain to drift silently to the asphalt and lie there with a soft thud. His companion, probably his wife, likely dressed in workman's coveralls might have remained in the vehicle. So far so good they must have thought.

Still in total darkness, the vehicle moved quietly farther up the road and stopped in front of the zoo office doors. The ignition was turned off and its two occupants remained silent looking around them, then perhaps at each other. One of them was the lead, the other merely another set of hands and eyes, there to follow instructions and keep a lookout. They may have been staring at each other with bright eyes, congratulating one another on their successful progress so far, with a glance and a smile, no words being necessary, or maybe they did none of that. Maybe they were anxious with nerves, rubbernecking.

The driver would have exited the vehicle. He would have reached into his workman's coveralls and pulled out another homemade key—a key he made himself. The key to the zoo office door. The man pushes the key in, and it works beautifully, slipping into the lock like a hand into a worn kid glove. The door is now open and the two burglars quickly and quietly unload their equipment, hauling it inside as silently as they can, careful not to make a sound.

Once the equipment was safely inside they moved the vehicle back down the access road to hide it from the Night Watchman, who worked also as a cage cleaner. In only a few minutes he would be making his rounds again, after cleaning out a number of small primate enclosures and laying out fresh straw.

The couple would have known from their research that the man would be cleaning out cages safely away from the zoo office for at least another thirty minutes. At that point, the couple would walk back to the zoo office and begin their task. Black plastic would be taped over the windows. Office furniture moved out of the way leaving room to work on the safe. All they'd need is a little time and a lot of luck to get it done right.

✳✳✳✳

What comes to mind when you hear the words *Jewel Thief?* Does it conjure up an image of tall handsome Cary Grant from the movie *To Catch a Thief*—a suave, sophisticated and debonair man living an exciting life alongside the character played by the beautiful Grace Kelly? Perhaps you think of the young handsome Robert Wagner in the TV series *It Takes a Thief?* Or maybe you think of a dashing man scaling rooftops and climbing in balcony windows to pull off a heist?

In my professional career as a police detective for the *Portland Police Bureau* and later as a hotel security executive working for the *Benson Hotel*, I encountered three jewel thieves. None however were young, handsome, or in any way dashing, but they *were* all men. And they were the kind of men you would *never* suspect would end up jewel thieves.

Charles Eugene Wright heisted $17,000 worth of diamonds in 1973, and then tried to sell them in Las Vegas. Poor "Charlie" Wright was chubby, almost obese, middle aged and balding. I thought he looked pretty good though in that orange prison jump-suit he ended up wearing—with my help. He had caused a lot of people a great deal of trouble by the time he was done.

William Wells Lewis, or as he was commonly known, *Billy Lewis,* was the most ingenious burglar of his time, active in the 1960s and 1970s and someone I actually admired quite a lot. I admired Billy because of how skilled he was in what he did. He turned safe cracking into an art form when it was a big issue for law enforcement at the time and one of our primary areas of focus.

This was during the years when stores were not open twenty-four-hours-a-day and grocery stores and other businesses, like plumbing supply stores, were often the target of burglars intent on getting at the store safe filled with cash, so they could bust it open and haul off the loot.

We were able to put Billy in prison for ten years for a safe burglary he pulled off at the Portland Zoo in July of 1969 when he was at the apex of his safe cracking abilities. Billy was the rare result of a kid whose father had been a small-time crook, a common pickpocket and burglar who wasn't very good and got caught more often than not. Billy grew up learning the various tricks of the trade from his dad, a man named Sam Lewis who was regularly in trouble with the Portland Police Bureau going as far back as 1943 when he tried to pickpocket another man, failed and was caught and promptly arrested and thrown in jail.

After many years of burglarizing, Billy got away with the biggest Portland jewelry and gold heist in my memory. The case was never officially solved but I *know* it was Billy who pulled it off. More on the details of *that* caper, later.

Billy, like the other jewel thief, Charles Eugene Wright, was not tall or handsome either. He wasn't bad looking, just kind of unprepossessing, neither bad nor good looking. He was average. In fact, all the jewel thieves I ever came across were exceptionally average and forgettable looking. They had average faces you see in a crowd and never remember, because they looked so ordinary. But Billy was a genius at lock picking, key making and safe burglary. He was a stealthy, patient and skilled burglar and when he wasn't cracking safes he tended bar at Billy Moe's *Gold Coin Lounge*—near Burnside Street, near The Stadium Fred Meyer's, which was a hangout for Portland gangsters, prostitutes, thieves and the Portland losers living on the edge, during that time in the 60s and 70s.

Billy also tended bar in Beaverton, at the *White Elephant* on Canyon Road. The building is still there, but it is now a car dealership. The building is more or less the same and still painted bright white, with the rounded front façade where the dance floor used to be. People drive by it all the time and have no clue what it used to be. But back in the free wheeling 1970s, it was Beaverton's own gangster hangout and a home for numerous nefarious characters up to no good while looking for female companionship. Billy was popular with the waitresses, sometimes giving them jewelry as gifts and according to one source he was a "great story teller," spinning entertaining tales that many folks weren't sure were true or not.

The third jewel thief I came to know was a man named Robert A. Bormes, a Westin Hotel executive who crossed my path when I was working as Director of Security for the Benson Hotel in downtown Portland in the early and middle 1980s. I had to work *backwards*, as an investigator, to figure out what Bormes, whom I came to call *Fast Bobby* behind his back, was really doing. Suffice it to say I never trusted Bormes, because he always lived beyond his means and he gave me a bad vibe. Fast Bobby was never my supervisor, but he did transfer into Portland from the Westin Hotel in Chicago to work as an executive assistant manager at the Benson Hotel, and so our paths crossed regularly.

In my appraisal of Fast Bobby, I came to learn Bobby, like many people I would encounter in my time was probably up to no good. I came to this conclusion long before I discovered what I believe happened at the Chicago hotel where he worked as an office manager, before he came to Portland, and where he had unlimited power, access and influence.

I learned of a large theft of diamonds from a safe vault located in the Westin Chicago Hotel in 1984 when I attended a Westin Hotel "security conference" in Kansas City Missouri in 1985. The loss at the Westin Hotel was over one million dollars and was a hot topic of conversation at the conference. The case had already been closed when it was a topic of discussion at the 1985 conference I attended, and Lloyds of London—the insurer of the diamonds, had already paid off the claim. No arrests were made and amazingly, no person was ever prosecuted for the theft.

I worked over ten years as a burglary detective and I knew the specifics of burglary: how it's done, who does it, and how to detect it, and even prevent burglary with things like pressure pads, cameras and other forms of surveillance. I knew burglary like the back of my hand. Though I did work as a homicide detective while employed with PPB, burglary really was my forte; hence my understanding of these three men and what motivated them to become burglars.

But let's go back to chubby Charlie Wright and how I came to know *him*. Charles Wright preferred to be called *Chuck*. Perhaps he thought it sounded more masculine than Charlie, but I never felt the nickname suited him. I encountered Chuck and his wife, Lou, when I rented an apartment in east Portland where they both worked as managers. It was obvious that Charlie's wife was the actual manager and Chuck simply worked as a traveling diamond salesman, as he was frequently leaving on sales trips with his little black bag full of precious cut diamonds.

Chuck wore a trendy gold wristwatch which I admired on more than one occasion. He offered to buy one for me through his connections one afternoon while we were chatting outside the apartment complex where we lived. As I was preparing to head to work, I agreed to his suggestion and handed him $100 in cash on the spot.

But Chuck was in no hurry to get me my watch. After waiting more than a month and reminding him with a telephone call that he still owed me a watch, he cheerfully promised to get it for me on his next sales trip. Another few weeks went by and my watch still was never delivered. I felt Charlie showed some ballsy lack of smarts when he continued to ignore me. Did he really think he could get away with conning a cop?

As a burglary detective, I was privy to the downtown pawn shop tickets that crossed my desk on a daily basis. Regularly checking the pawn shops for stolen merchandise was a burglary detective's responsibility, and we took it seriously. Al Vigna and I, along with Bob Chappell, and Mike O'Leary were expected to make visits in person to the local pawn shops. That part of the job could be tedious but we all had to do it, and there wasn't a week that went by that I didn't make at least three trips to various downtown pawn shops to look over their records. I had to eyeball the potentially stolen merchandise and compare their records to my lists of items taken in burglaries.

We were expected to recover stolen property and talk to the shop owners, who were often more than aware they were buying stolen jewelry, cameras, electronics and collectables. In this way, we got to know the criminals' names and locations and created files on them, along with learning about the general character of the pawn shop owners.

Some of them went by the book and others were as crooked as the winding road to the top of Pikes Peak in Colorado.

One fall afternoon, I noted that Mr. Charles Eugene Wright had pawned some diamonds recently and yet had not retrieved them from that particular pawn shop. Because they were still in hock I came to two conclusions: I guessed that Charlie had gone on another trip out of town, and I surmised the diamonds came from his sample case and were pawned to give him the extra cash he would need for the trip and any recreation he may have wanted to indulge in while out of town and away from his wife.

So, as a police detective, I played my hole card. I put a "police hold" on the diamonds. Charlie would have to speak to *me* to get his diamonds back. This was something I did occasionally when I needed more time to investigate a case, and it was as simple as making a phone call to the pawn shop owner or his associates and telling them which diamonds or jewelry they could *not* sell or release until further notice from me. *Those* items would be removed from the display case and held in the back room.

A few days later, as expected, the detective desk clerk, Mrs. Emma Jozaitis, (widow of my first partner Frank Jozaitis) told me there was a Mr. Wright waiting to speak with me in the waiting area outside my office in downtown Portland. I chuckled to myself and asked Emma to allow Mr. Wright access to the Burglary Detail. This meant he had to be buzzed past security and into my office on the second floor of the building overlooking Third Avenue (which is now the troubled Westshore Apartments, home to low income and disabled Portlanders).

Chuck was the picture of humility and quite apologetic as he came into my office and sat timidly at my desk with my new watch dangling from his extended hand. "Uh, sorry, it took so long, Don," he said, "I've been kinda busy." I stood up, walked around my desk with a smile on my face and strapped on my new watch without a word. It was a beauty, a Bulova Accutron skeleton watch with a sharp looking black leather band and a bright green transparent face. I said nothing, making Chuck wait a moment, in nervous anticipation as I admired the watch, holding my arm out so I could see it glitter in the sunlight coming in through the windows.

After I had placed the hold on the diamonds the week before, when he tried to buy them back he was told by the owner, he'd have to speak to "Detective DuPay first." I knew Chuck was surprised at the long reach of the law, as delivered by me, but that's how it was done and he had only himself to blame. I enjoyed a long delicious moment of one-upmanship as I admired my new watch, and then asked Charlie how I could help him? He bowed his head and asked politely if I could "please release the diamonds" in the pawnshop so he could get them and head home.

 I sat back down at my desk, pulled out the pad of release forms from my desk drawer, and signed the release slip, handing it over to him. As he reached for the slip, I playfully pulled it away for a short moment, and then handed it back to him with a chuckle. "There you go Charlie, we're even now. And remember, I *am* a cop." Charlie nodded his head, but said nothing, avoiding eye contact with me. The last I saw of Chuck that day was his overly ample rear-end waddling out the burglary office door, bent over and defeated. But being pragmatic, I felt he had done it to himself so I didn't feel sorry for the guy one bit.

Fast forward a few months later to different home environs. Suffice it to say my wife and I moved to a better apartment and lost track of Chuck, but now that I knew he was *not* a very smart thief, I kept him on my detectives' radar. I hadn't heard anything about him in months until one day the burglary office received a teletype from the Las Vegas police department. They were inquiring as to where a Mr. Charles Eugene Wright from Portland may have obtained $17,000 in cut diamonds he pawned in Vegas?

Remember I said I kept Chuck on my radar?

I *knew* he had been working as a jewelry salesman at an upscale jewelry store in Portland's Lloyd Center Mall for some time. I telephoned the jewelry store and discovered chubby Charlie had not shown up for work and had disappeared with a lot of diamonds only a day or two ago. They were wondering where he and *their* diamonds had disappeared to, and were just about to call the authorities, the man breathlessly told me, and could the Portland Police Bureau help, he suddenly wanted to know.

It seemed Chuck had *not* figured out how the pawnshop detectives worked and had stuck his foot "in it" again. But this time Chuck was in some serious shit. Interstate transportation of stolen property is a serious federal crime. Chuck was arrested in Vegas and extradited back to Oregon by several FBI agents and all the diamonds he had stolen were recovered and shipped back to Portland.

Again, I felt Charlie looked good in prison orange and I felt good about him doing serious prison time. A week later, the FBI awarded me a letter of commendation for Charlie's arrest, thanking me for my work on the case, and how it led to the recovery of $17,000 worth of stolen diamonds. (PPB Personnel File).

William Wells Lewis was a different kind of burglar. Billy was the epitome of a skilled safe burglar, a "box-man" or a "mechanic" as we called the good ones. Billy's disguise was also perfect in that he was the average looking everyman. No handsome dashing TV burglar in Billy. Billy was white, about six feet tall, with short dark hair and weighed around 175 pounds. He had the face of a school teacher, banker or a college professor, totally forgettable for the most part. Billy's skill at picking locks, making keys and opening complicated safes protected by sophisticated alarms never showed in his face or demeanor. He was innately humble and knew the value of being completely low-key and staying under the radar. Billy was *smart!*

But before I tell you about how Billy stole thousands in jewelry and gold coins from the H&B pawn shop and how he did it, I have to finish telling you about the other masterful burglary Billy almost got away with. It demonstrated the ingenuity and skill level of the consummate thief who plans, in detail, how they're going to commit their crime and get away with it.

And that crime was the notorious 1969 Portland Zoo burglary.

****

The heat from the torched open metal safe at the Portland Zoo had hardly dissipated when my partner Detective John Wayne Wesson and I received a call from Willard Mayfield, the president of the Zoological Society. The man was astounded that the entire proceeds of the 4th of July weekend were gone. All the money from the rides, the concession stands and gate fees were just simply gone. Someone had busted into the safe and taken it all.

When I arrived at the zoo office that morning, the heat emanating from the torched open safe was still warm to the touch, and the office where the safe was located was a complete mess. There was water all over the floor as well as the white powdery "fire clay" and thick black plastic which still covered the windows. Chairs and office furniture were strewn about to clear the room in order to make space for the burglars to get close to the safe. The most astounding part was when the Zoo director told us that the office door was *locked* when he arrived. This meant the burglars had made a key *prior* to breaking in and had locked the door behind them when they finished, nice and tidy. It was hard not to be impressed by that little touch. Billy thought of everything.

A back access road from Washington Park to the "zoo grounds proper" had been chained shut and secured with a padlock. There were tire tracks on the zoo side of the chain, indicating the chain had to have been unlocked before any vehicles could go through. This aspect of the burglary had confused the now hand-wringing president, Mr. Mayfield, who had shown us the fresh tire tracks, hoping the tracks would tell us something. Only John Wesson and I knew the significance of this signature and what it revealed.

We *knew* who had done this burglary when we were told the office door had been locked on the way out, and the chain link padlock relocked. There was only one man who *could* have done it and we in Burglary *all* knew his name.

The night security guard had seen nothing at all, he said, and all the doors were locked when he did his rounds, including the gate so he would never have thought anything was amiss. Upon close questioning of the guard it was revealed his duties were mostly cleaning out soiled cages, more of a pooper scooper than a real security guard.

As Detective John Wesson and I stood in the office, looking over the burglarized remains of the safe and listening to Mr. Mayfield ramble, we looked at each other and I could tell we were both thinking the same thing. We didn't have to say a word, it was mental telepathy. John and I both knew there was only *one* man capable of making keys to unlock *and* relock doors and padlocks *and* cut open a safe with an acetylene torch and that man was of course *William Wells Lewis.*

We knew Billy had been active since a recent burglary at the downtown H&B pawn shop owned by Lou Tobin and that thousands in jewelry and gold coins had been stolen. Now our job was to prove that it was *Billy* who had done the zoo burglary.

Back to the details: From the amount of equipment the burglars left on the job—acetylene torch, hoses, tanks, a large electric power drill, duct tape, scotch tape, a large roll of black industrial plastic, some of which was still taped to the windows, a couple of thirty six inch steel pry bars and a metal chisel and wooden mallet, it was obvious a truck or van had likely been used to haul it all up to the zoo.

They had to have unlocked the office door, unloaded their equipment, stashed the truck and relocked the door upon entering. The pry bars were used to force open the wire mesh gate to the office area where the safe was located. Next, the black plastic was taped over the windows to keep anyone from looking in and to hide the intermittent yellow flashes the acetylene torch would make. That there were no fingerprints revealed the burglars had worn gloves.

The chisel was used to cut through the thin grey metal skin covering the top of the safe revealing four inches of clay which insulated the safe from fire. Chiseling and scraping out the powdery fire clay covered the small room with a fine white powder, some of it turning to sludge in the areas where there was water on the floor. It gave the scene an ominous quality, rather like the interior of a long abandoned, damp mausoleum from a B horror film.

Once the fire clay was removed, the hole exposed a one inch steel plate protecting the cash inside. The heavy-duty drill was then used to drill a hole through that protective layer of thick steel. A waste paper basket from the office was filled with water and the water was poured into the hole directly, probably with a funnel, saturating the green money bags with water. The front of the safe where the door was located was covered snugly with tape to prevent the water from seeping out the cracks.

Next the torch was lit and the flame adjusted with the correct amount of oxygen and acetylene needed to cut through the steel. One can just imagine the sputtering of the intense flame hitting the cold water and the resultant steam escaping and dissipating above the burglar's heads. It must have been a spectacular sight. Two burglars staring at the steaming flame through welder's goggles as the steam mixed with the white fire clay, and hoping no one would hear or discover them at their task. While they sweated and dripped—adrenaline pumping through their systems, they must have been stressed and on high alert.

A six inch hole was cut through the top steel plate and then the plug removed. The rest was easy. The torch was extinguished, put aside and abandoned. Then they reached inside and pulled out the bags of money. With all the cash now theirs and safely inside the green money bags, they unlocked the office door, and exited, relocking the door from the outside, leaving behind all of their equipment. Now, all they had to do was hurry to their truck, hop over the chain and sneak quietly away into the dim forest of Washington Park and anonymity, forever, right?

Well—almost.

My boss in burglary always told me that "most crooks catch themselves." Mostly because "they aren't very smart," he told me. Consequently they break the one law which can't be broken with impunity—the law of averages. My boss was Detective Lieutenant Myron Warren, head of the burglary and pawn shop detectives, and the organizer of the elite *PPB Safe Burglary Detail*.

Lt. Warren was widely recognized as a charismatic leader and one of the most knowledgeable burglary supervisors on the west coast. He was the original organizer of the *West Coast Regional Safe Burglary Annual Conference*, held yearly in Eugene, Oregon. In the middle 1960s sophisticated gangs of safe burglars roamed the Western United States; these "yeggs" as they were called, routinely terrorized large chain grocery stores such as *Safeway* and *Thriftway* on a regular basis. The burglars were free to spend an entire night inside a store because almost all large grocery stores were dark at night with no overnight employees working. The pickings were easy and the rewards great, sometimes getting as much as $40,000 to $50,000 dollars over a weekend take.

The members of the safe burglary squad that I was a part of were seasoned detectives in their late forties and early fifties.

Detectives like Ladd Hunt, Bob Chappell, Al Vigna, and John Wayne Wesson made up this elite group of investigators. And then there was me, who they all called "the kid" because I was so young. After being promoted to detective in November of 1967, at the age of 31 and working burglary cases for a couple of years, I attracted enough attention that Myron Warren personally handpicked me to join the prestigious Safe Detail, a real honor for someone as young as I was at the time.

My evaluation forms consistently indicated it was my attention to detail and habit of being "aggressive and determined" which made Warren decide to take a chance on me. He had watched me work my assigned cases in Burglary and was impressed by the total number of cases I cleared through arrest—meaning when one burglar was arrested and interrogated, they might confess to *other* burglaries and we could clear *those* crimes as well, creating a kind of Domino effect. Warren assigned me to the *Safe Squad*, where I was soon accepted and affectionately labeled "the kid."

After the zoo burglary was completed—it was only a few days after this particularly daring caper—that a longshoreman discovered something unusual. He was eating his lunch; innocently sitting on the dock with his feet dangling over the edge of Terminal One in St. Johns. He was looking out over the scenic Willamette River when he happened to notice something bumping up against the pier. The object appeared to be a military duffel bag about five feet long and a dark forest green color. Putting aside his sandwich, he extended a long pole with a grappling hook on the end that he had next to him, and dragged up the duffel bag. Curious, he pulled the soaking bag onto the pier and looked inside, retrieving several green money bags marked, *Portland Zoo*. The man knew something wasn't right and immediately called the police who arrived in less than thirty minutes.

Within an hour the wet bag was drying out on a large table in the Safe Detail office of the Portland Police Bureau, with the bedraggled contents spread out over the table, also drying. We spread out the empty bags and several pieces of paper to dry, plus two pairs of overalls worn by the burglars, two pairs of heavy leather welding gloves, and two pairs of dark welding goggles, but all without any kind of identifying marks. Finally, we dried out a pair of brown leather loafers with crepe rubber soles.

I remember as I sat at the table, I picked up the loafers and examined them. Clearly visible in the crevices of the soft rubber soles, I saw small green fibers. The fibers would eventually be sent to our criminalists to be examined under a microscope and perhaps even identified and connected to their original location.

On a slip of wet paper were some written numerical figures showing how much money had been in each money bag including a small amount which had been burned. It totaled about $10,000 dollars—the amount the zoo claimed to have lost! Turning the scrap of wet paper over, we saw it was a pay stub made out to one Marjorie Lewis.

Marjorie was the wife of Billy Lewis!

Now, for the first time Detective John Wesson and I knew for sure, the burglar *was* Billy Lewis and we had him! We had Billy *cold*! The rest of the day was taken up by the tedious process of getting a search warrant for his house (of course we knew where he lived) and waiting to have it approved and signed by a judge.

No one was home when we arrived at the Lewis residence, a two story older home located in the St John's area of Portland and only about two miles from the pier at Terminal One where the duffle bag was found floating. After making sure the house was empty Detective Wesson and I found the mother lode of evidence we had been looking for in Billy's upstairs bedroom, which also served as his locksmith shop. I noticed right away the color of the shag carpet on the stairway! It was a wild lime green color, commonly in vogue in the 1970s.

"Hey wait, John?"

"Yeah, what is it?"

"Look at this green carpet, here!" I said. "I'll bet the fibers on the bottom of those loafers match *this* carpet!"

"I bet you're right, Don!"

"Let's get it checked out."

As John Wesson chuckled and we began walking up the stairs, I pinched off some samples of the carpet fibers to match against the fibers in the crevices of the crepe rubber sole shoes. After stuffing the fibers in a clear plastic evidence bag, rather like a sandwich bag, to be sent to the criminalists later for inspection, I continued up the stairs with John behind me.

We walked into the bedroom and were delighted with what we found. There was a profusion of key blanks, notching files, a key cutting machine and Billy's lesson plans with his full name and grades from the instructor who graded his home study locksmith courses.

Billy was an A student in key cutting, lock picking and making keys from impressions—which is a very difficult skill to master. Making keys by *impression* is a big challenge and not everyone can do it. I knew that this was the way Billy had made the keys to the padlock which secured the chain across the zoo back road. And that this was how he had made the key to the zoo office door.

We took the locksmith lesson plans, and the key cutting machine as evidence, tagged it all and secured the house. We hurried to the Identification lab in the main police station downtown in what they called "the police block" and stood looking over the shoulder of the criminalist while he examined the fibers found in the soles of the shoes with the fiber samples I collected from the stairway covered in green shag. After about ten minutes of staring at the fibers through a comparison microscope, he sighed dramatically, pushed his chair back and looked up at both of us with a smug smile. "The fibers in the shoe sole are the *same* as the fibers from the carpet. It's a match, guys!"

Detective Wesson and I nearly cheered as we looked at each other and knew instantly what we had to do next. John and I often had that ability to understand what the other was thinking, without saying a word and that instance with the criminalist was yet another time when John and I could read each other perfectly.

We had to find Billy and arrest him before he returned home to discover we had already been at his place and he could try to run. My adrenaline was pumping and I was excited. John was excited too, I could tell, yet we tried to maintain some professional dignity and composure. Standing next to each other, we were all smiles—smiles we couldn't control. We both knew we had Billy.

After discussing where Billy Lewis might be at, we decided to check out Bill's Gold Coin, a restaurant and local gangster hangout located at 20th and West Burnside where Billy worked as a bartender. We drove our unmarked car to Bill's Gold Coin and parked unobtrusively in the back. The front parking area was filled with Cadillac's, Mercedes, and Jaguar's backed in parking spots so the front of their luxury cars faced the street—a signature of the Gold Coin that let everyone know it was a gangster hangout. And indeed it was. They were out in force that day.

With stern, serious looks on our faces John and I entered the front door and brushed past the Maître D, who had been standing there with menus in his hands. He looked after us uneasily as we swept past. Once inside, we paused for a moment, looking around, and surveying the darkened interior. There were patrons eating and talking and the bar had not one empty seat. But it became obvious things would go smoothly for us as Billy was sitting at the bar gently nursing a drink, which I later learned was his favorite, Cutty Sark Scotch.

Billy was sipping his drink with not a care in the world it seemed. I approached him on his right and John approached on his left and together we crowded against him simultaneously. As he sat up in alarm, I whispered in his ear: *"Billy Lewis? You're un-*

der arrest for burglarizing the Portland Zoo." He stiffened for a moment, and then leaned back on the bar stool, in mild shock and disgust as we quickly pulled his hands behind his back and snapped on the cuffs. He offered no resistance, his arms limp at his sides, but a grim look passed over his face and his eyes became darkly angry. Clearly, he had not been expecting *this!*

The unmistakable metallic sound of the handcuffs ratcheting together seemed to change the ambiance in the restaurant immediately. During my career with PPB, I found it put everything and everyone into slow motion. Conversations stopped mid-sentence, heads turned. Ice cubes stopped clinking in drink glasses and all eyes watched as two stern faced detectives hustled one of their favorite sons out of the door in cuffs. In an instant Billy was jerked from the oblivion of his relaxing Scotch with friends to the stark reality of the cold steel handcuffs and how those cuffs would change his life. He didn't realize it then but due to his own carelessness, his life was about to change in some dramatic and unpleasant ways.

Even while serving time in an Oregon prison, I knew Billy would be okay. Men like Billy were always revered by the criminal element. They were smarter than most, lifetime criminals and always had a following of interested men who wanted to learn from them. I wasn't worried about Billy. He'd be fine while he did his time.

We stuffed Billy in the back seat of the unmarked car, a tan 1967 Plymouth sedan. John Wesson crowded into the backseat with him while I started the car and adjusted the rearview mirror so I could observe both Billy and John. It took me about five minutes weaving through traffic to drive from 20th and West

Burnside to the old Police Headquarters at SW 3rd and Pine.

There was no conversation of any kind in the car. No small talk and no smiling. The silence seemed magnified by the sound of the engine running and I could see Billy sitting motionless in the back, looking out the window sullenly. He may have been thinking these two coppers had nothing on him because he knew he'd tossed his gear and notations deep in the Willamette River, or perhaps he'd had someone else do it for him. Watching him in the rearview mirror I saw a certain smugness and a series of fluttering, half-smile smirks drift across his face. Perhaps he was thinking we had him only on *suspicion* and didn't have any concrete evidence. He sure was wrong.

Detective Wesson's demeanor was firm and morose. And I shared his attitude, but as we were not inclined to boast, push or antagonize a suspect we knew we had by the shorts, we said nothing on the drive to Headquarters. We had caught one of the cleverest and most efficient safe crackers the state of Oregon had ever seen. We knew we had Billy cold, and that he was on his way to prison. The ride from Bill's Gold Coin to third and Pine was just the first leg of Billy's journey which would take him directly to the Oregon State Penitentiary in Salem.

At Police Headquarters, I parked the Plymouth sedan in the basement parking area reserved for detective cars and stepped out of the car. Our serious non-smiling and silent demeanor continued as I helped Billy out of the back seat, into the elevator and up to the lobby floor. Crowding him between us we walked him up the lobby stairs, each holding him by the elbow, and directed him to the second floor detective office. Mrs. Emma Jozaitis was manning the reception area, and buzzed us in with a hesitant smile.

I picked room B for no particular reason and ushered Billy in the door, guiding him to a chair pushed up against the wall, and motioned for him to sit down. The three interview rooms all looked the same, generic looking, rundown spaces with no windows. The room was eight feet by twelve feet, about the same size as a jail cell and just as claustrophobic. The walls were painted a pale institutional green with no decorative framed prints or calendars on the walls. An old fashioned wood table scarred by decades of pencil and ink doodling sat in the middle of the room with three hardwood chairs nearby for seating.

The chairs looked ancient but sturdy, with the finish worn off in each seat. A metal tag was affixed to the back of the chairs with a six digit stock number and lettering that proclaimed the chair to be the Property of the City of Portland.

I removed my handcuffs from Billy's wrists and secured them over my belt on the left side where I usually carried them, waiting for John Wesson to retrieve two evidence bags from the detective evidence locker in the safe detail office. I stared sternly at Billy still not speaking; watching his facial expressions go from smirks and small grins to a look of confusion and back again.

His mind was racing. It was obvious.

I knew what was going on. Billy was certain the evidence against him was at the bottom of the Willamette River and probably presumed we were just going to pressure him into a confession with nothing to go on. I remained silent and continued staring at Billy just to make him uncomfortable, looking him directly in the eyes and willing him to a staredown. He gazed at me with something like anger on his face but caved after only a few seconds and looked away.

After about five minutes Detective Wesson re-entered the small room with three clear evidence bags, handing them to me without a word. I opened the first bag and removed a pair of brown leather loafers. They were a little stiff from soaking in the Willamette for a few hours, I set them carefully in front of Billy, with the rubber soles facing up. Next I opened the second bag containing the green shag carpeting samples I had obtained from his house. I opened the third bag and removed the now dry paycheck stub with the cash accounting written in blue ink on the back, including the money that was burned by the acetylene torch, and watched as the shock of recognition slowly spread over Billy's face.

The silence was thick—soupy thick—as John and I continued looking down at the evidence before us and then back at Billy. Now, the smirks were on our faces. Billy's eyes continued to stare at the table, looking from one object to the other and back again. He realized what he was seeing. Finally, he took a raspy deep breath, let it out slowly and sank back into the hard backed chair. He looked deflated—as if his clothing had suddenly become two sizes too large. There were three people in that room and they *all* knew William Wells Lewis was headed to prison.

"I suppose you wanna know where we got your shoes and your wife's pay stub?" I asked casually, by way of breaking the ice and starting a conversation. I knew Billy must be dying to know the answer, but he didn't respond to my question, nodding only a barely perceptible yes.

"Well, Billy, a longshoreman eating his lunch down at Terminal one spotted a bag floating in the river and fished it out for us. If he hadn't been eating his ham and cheese sandwich at that moment you might still be drinking at the Gold Coin, right now."

"Uh huh?" Billy said sullenly, his jaw clenching over and over, his eyes angry and seething.

"What'd you do with the money?" I asked, pressing my luck. Billy slowly leaned back into his chair and pushed his feet into the floor, getting as far away from me as possible.

"I'm not talkin' to you guys," he said quietly, gently shaking his head back and forth, indicating no, he would not cooperate.

"Who was the other burglar? Was it your wife, Marjorie?"

"Not talkin' to you guys!" he repeated quietly, looking down.

"Where'd you learn to use a torch like that, Billy?"

"Not talking. You're wastin' your time."

Billy had a closed off seething look on his face. We knew he was far too smart to talk so we put him back in handcuffs and took him up to the fifth floor jail and booked him in for Burglary. Within the month a circuit court judge sent William Wells Lewis to the Oregon State Penitentiary for ten long years. Detective Wesson and I felt a great deal of professional pride in convicting a prolific and intelligent safe burglar, and I remembered what my boss Myron Warren once told me: "Most crooks *catch* themselves because they're just not very smart."

Even the smart ones make stupid, preventable mistakes. Billy Lewis may have thought anything tossed in the river would sink to the bottom, if he had done it himself, cutting the bottom of the bag out so it would sink. My feeling is he may have asked his wife to dispose of the evidence, instead. She probably would not have thought to cut out the bottom of the bag.

Even a fairly new duffel bag will float, especially if it's filled with air and objects like paper and shoes. Maybe it was the law of averages that caught Billy. Or maybe it was just his karma. But if that curious lunching longshoreman hadn't noticed a floating green duffle bag and dragged it out of the Willamette River, we would never have caught Lewis for his caper, and the knowledge of that must have bothered Billy. If only he had been a little more careful, he must have lamented. If only he had thrown away the duffel bag himself.

****

When I left PPB in 1978, I resigned for documented health reasons and under my personal doctor's advice. He'd been talking to me for years about quitting, telling me the job would end up killing me. I had abnormally high blood pressure by the time I was 35, and a serious bleeding ulcer, not to mention periods of deep depression I tried to hide from everyone, including myself.

Eventually, in 1980 I began working for the Benson Hotel, which was the premier hotel in downtown Portland. The management had unwittingly hired an old street cop and an experienced investigator. That fact would one day prove quite beneficial to the Benson Hotel.

Sometimes I felt the general manager regretted that I had been hired because I made many changes that involved upgrading fire safety measures and the rampant kitchen food and wine theft was stopped in its tracks under my watch as well.

While working at PPB, I spent years interrogating suspects, being lied to by experts and assessing and evaluating personalities. I did the same when I was surrounded by a whole new crop of personalities working at the fashionable Benson hotel. The General Manager, Chet, a balding Beta personality and son of the founder of Westin Hotels, found he was in his position only because his father had put him there. Chet was over his head in a job he was not qualified for or even interested in doing. But he *was* teachable. He spent most of his workday hiding in his walnut paneled office. He wouldn't even come out for bathroom breaks, but that was because he had his own in-office bathroom.

The executive chef was an overweight, sarcastic and misogynistic food Nazi who looked down on all other mortals as lesser beings and basically inconsequential. He terrorized and bullied his underlings, particularly women kitchen employees, yelled his displeasure with a snarl on his face and all with his booming voice and thick German accent.

Think *Gordon Ramsey* of today. Think Iron Chef.

Fast forward a couple of years later, when Robert Bormes, former office manager of the downtown Westin Hotel in the city of Chicago transferred to the Benson Hotel in Portland. It was a promotion for him from being the office manager in Chicago, to that of an Executive Assistant Manager at the Benson Hotel.

When Bormes was first introduced to all of the department heads at the weekly staff meeting, he was well dressed in an expensive off-green sharkskin suit. He was well spoken and convinced us that he was a "team player." He even went so far as to say we were all a "family," which is a common emotional ploy among business owners, and supervisors who want employees to be loyal, obedient, and even accept low pay. Make them think they're really needed and they might be more inclined to overlook unsatisfactory working conditions, as they're part of a "family."

Though Bormes was new to the position, he also seemed eager to learn and cooperate with the rest of us. Bobby had an easy smile, and perfect teeth. When he frowned, his eyebrows furrowed up towards his thinning hairline in an earnest manner. But there was something about Bormes that bothered me. He looked, to my experienced eye, to be a true-blue phony.

I thought he was a little too smiley, and a little too slick in his appearance, demeanor and congeniality. He seemed disingenuous and something about him put him on my immediate radar. Doing a little checking of my own I discovered he and his wife rented an expensive waterfront highrise apartment. The apartment cost more than his monthly salary. Fast Bobby was living far beyond his means, and I knew in all likelihood what that meant.

In the next few weeks I overheard snippets of conversation from other Benson employees while they were eating in the staff lunchroom about the new Assistant Manager. The consensus was that Bob Bormes was a pretty good guy—he was easygoing, always smiling it seemed and he let his employees do their work without riding them. Everyone seemed to like him. Oh, and his wife had money. I had heard that a lot, but rumors about such things are easy to start, you just tell a lie about yourself, and the rest takes care of itself. People are always willing to talk. I was interested in the employee's evaluation of Bormes, as my only interaction with him was to smile cordially as we passed each other in the corridors. As a result, I was an avid listener to whoever wanted to share their opinions on Bormes.

But strange things began happening. During the next few months his wife made three roundtrip airline flights to Chicago and back. "To visit her mother I heard," one young woman in the lunchroom told me. My old cop radar was still pinging—something wasn't right about Bormes. He and the missus were living in an apartment he couldn't afford on his own earnings, she traveled a lot and they regularly ate out at expensive restaurants and wore only the best threads. Maybe his wife did have money or was that just a convenient lie to cover for the real reasons they could afford all those trips?

Roundtrip airfare to Chicago was not cheap either, particularly during the 1980s. I wondered where his money was coming from and how he was able to afford such a lavish lifestyle. Two plus two was not adding up to four in this scenario. Not with the way Bobby and his wife were spending so much money. I never mentioned my suspicions to Chet, the manager, because I thought it would just confuse and frighten him. In many respects Chet was clueless and knew next to nothing about the human condition, crime or criminals, least of all white collar criminals who were sophisticated, so I never bothered to confide in him.

I had *never* trusted Bormes, though, not from the time I first met him and that would not change. I spoke to him only when necessary and never shared information with him, even when he tried to engage with me I maintained a discernible distance. I wasn't a cop anymore so I couldn't stuff him in a vacant room and interrogate him, I had to observe him from afar and trust my instincts were correct from all my years of watching crooks and predators and learning how they speak, move, think and manipulate people.

It was probably a good thing for Bormes, but I refused to engage with him in any way other than to briefly discuss professional duties. As the work weeks passed, Bormes was not my primary focus at the Benson Hotel. Other pressing matters demanded my attention, like possible drug dealing in hotel rooms and "lily wavers," harassing grannies and middle aged women traveling from out of state.

I was also busy bringing the hotel up to the modern safety and security standards of the current hotel industry, such as outfitting the entire building with smoke detectors. When I had been hired in 1980 I'd noticed that there were *no* smoke detectors of *any* kind in the hotel, not one, which surprised me. The lack of smoke detectors was a disaster waiting to happen. I knew I had to save the Benson from possible fire.

I waited a few months after being hired, and started pressuring Chet to approve the needed upgrades, explaining to him how fires being averted in the previous decades must have been like some kind of bizarre miracle, what with the two large kitchens, one located on the first floor and the other in the basement, it was only a matter of time before a serious kitchen fire caused some serious damage, or even loss of life.

I told Chet that installing smoke detectors in *every* single room was not only necessary, it was essential to the Benson Hotel's continued existence and there was absolutely *no* way around it. When he tried to argue with me, which he did, citing the expense, I warned him that a fire at the Benson would be a catastrophe and that *he* would be held accountable for it and blamed. I shrugged my shoulders and reminded him *he* was the manager and that I was only trying to help him, but that I was not in a position to take no for an answer. As a former police officer who understood fire code and the law, it was *my* obligation to make sure that the hotel was safe, whether *he* approved of it or not.

Another serious concern was modernizing their way of handling guest room key control. Chet never seemed to understand the importance of key control. I had to explain the process to him repeatedly and the legal reasons *why* it was imperative that key control be upgraded. That and creating an *Emergency Response Team* of first responders was another one of my serious safety issues, so as I was busy arranging that. The upgrades were funded and actually happened, behind my back, Chet would find any reason to delay the process.

It required, after Chet balked a couple of times, me explaining the possibility of the Fire Department coming to look over each room, at *my* invitation of course. In time, Chet saw the light of day and he got together the money.

All during this time, though, Bormes had *never* left my radar completely.

****

Years later, in 1985, Westin Hotels convened a security manager's weeklong conference at their premier Westin hotel in Kansas City, Kansas. The Westin corporate office deemed it necessary that all security directors for Westin hotels attend, and that included me. When Chet received the news I would be attending the conference, that I was required to attend, and the Benson would pay all my expenses, he wasn't happy. Later, when I visited his office to receive my voucher money and airline tickets, we talked about my forthcoming trip to Kansas and he couldn't disguise his sullen displeasure.

Chet's continual worrying about hotel expenditures was legendary among the staff, and it annoyed me to no end. To me Chet seemed cheap and I never liked cheap people. He always waited until the very last minute to sign the purchase order slips so department heads could get their necessary supplies, like wine, linen, cleaning supplies or even fruits and cheeses. It was ridiculous. The cooks were often upset with Chet because he wouldn't regularly sign purchase orders for standard items like flour or sugar, or butter. How could a chef cook for patrons of the Benson Hotel without flour, sugar or butter to create pies, cakes or pasta with?

I remember one memorable occasion when I ran out of paper clips for my office. I submitted a purchase order, delivering it to his mailbox at the front desk, and handing it to the desk clerk. Chet had to have received it, but apparently he refused to sign it, as a week went by and I heard nothing. I learned later from the purchase officer, Janet, as we were having coffee in my office one day, that Chet had indeed *refused* to pay for the paper clips.

I was instantly furious. And though Janet was disgusted, she was also mildly bemused. Chet was refusing to pay for nickel and dime costs for simple office supplies like paper clips and Scotch tape. How was I supposed to do my job without paper clips or other office supplies I might need, I demanded, looking across my desk at Janet.

"The guy lives in Lake Oswego and the company pays him over $200 a month to have a car but he can't cough up some small change for some goddamn paperclips for the director of security? What's wrong with this guy? Does he *really* think he's saving the Benson money by not buying *paper clips*?!"

"I know, Don. He drives me batty, too."

"Yeah, well I've got an idea!"

I ended up buying my own paper clips for less than five dollars at an office supply store on Grand Avenue. The next day, I presented Chet with the receipt to be reimbursed to me personally. He was standing near the front desk chatting up a particularly pretty London Grill hostess. I walked up to him, smiled good-naturedly and handed him the receipt without a word. He looked puzzled as he said, "What's up Don?" But I had already turned my back and was strolling back to my office. Later that afternoon, I found a crisp five dollar bill paper clipped to a Post It Note, (with a paperclip) with his signature and a scrawled *Thank You* on it. Apparently, *he* had a sufficient supply of paper clips and now I did, too.

I had always envisioned that Chet had a fear his father was always looking over his shoulder watching the ever evolving hotel expenditures list get longer and longer with a scowl of disapproval on his lined face, but back to the story about the conference.

As Chet signed the voucher that day, and handed the airline tickets to me in a large white envelope, so I could fly to the conference, I judged from the frown on his face that he was already mentally wringing his hands regarding yet another expense on the ledger. But he handed me the envelope with a halfhearted smile and a falsely cheerful, "Good luck, Don, and uh, have fun!" I breezed out of his office with a perfunctory wave, my face expressionless, and a spring in my step. I was looking forward to the conference, having attended many such conferences when I was a detective with PPB and I was glad to be getting away from Chet, *and* Portland.

The event in Kansas City was educational for the many security supervisors present who attended. The industry was rapidly changing and we needed to stay on top of things. Some people might not understand the importance of these kinds of conferences but they are integral to staying abreast of new technology and improvements in whatever profession you find yourself in. Having attended many conferences on burglary when I was a detective, I knew how important the lectures and seminars were and how much you could gain from them.

You quickly learned that in the hotel business, the stereotypical "hotel dicks" or "hotel detectives" from the 1940s or 1950s were a thing of the past and had probably always been useless or at least of little value. They were often depicted as sitting in the hotel lobby pretending to read a newspaper. They would glance over the top of the sports page, hoping to locate any suspicious looking *working women* or transients looking for a handout so they could buy a bottle of *Night Train* or a pack of smokes from a sympathetic widow or young naive housewife traveling from out of town.

The hotel industry was changing and one important case underscored that fact perfectly: American pop singer *Connie Francis* was raped in a Howard Johnson motel in Westbury New York in November of 1974. Her rapist entered her room "through a faulty sliding door" at around 4:00 am, overpowered her and raped her at knife point.

He tied Francis to a chair which he left tipped over, and covered her with a mattress and a suitcase, leaving her on the floor, nude, traumatized and helpless and then silently left the room, but not before he stole her mink coat and some of her jewelry. This left Francis on her back, but after struggling for over half an hour, she made her way to the phone and called her long-time secretary who was sleeping in the room next door.

In the lawsuit, the court decided the hotel had failed to maintain their *"duty of care."* The courts came to the determination that hotels *must* anticipate risks for their clients and take care to *prevent* them from coming to harm. Ultimately, Connie Francis was awarded $2.5 million dollars in damages and her husband Joseph Garzilli was awarded $150,000 for "Loss of services of his wife" which alluded to their sexual relationship and any subsequent changes. This *was* 1974 and insensitive language like that is not surprising considering the time, but the case was historic for the large sum of monies awarded to Francis and her husband.

The Connie Francis ruling and the huge award she received rocked the hotel industry and essentially prompted the gathering of security officials on a regular basis, to such conferences as the one I attended in 1985. It was educational for all who attended, and we learned several things that were crucial to successful hotel management. We learned the term *reasonable care* came to mean:

1.) Control of the proliferation or theft of guest room keys.

2.) Fire safety, (smoke detectors in each room and a sprinkler system).

3.) An Emergency Response Team responsible for calls of smoke or fire, with master keys, fire extinguishers and pack-set radios to communicate with the hotel operator to direct first responders to specific locations in the hotel.

The US courts were clear that if the *"duty of care"* is breached in any way, the injured party *may* sue for monetary damages and be awarded them, depending on each individual case brought to the courts attention. Hotel security managers were now Risk Managers charged with managing and ameliorating all dangers to the potentially vulnerable hotel guests, and this meant *women* and their safety, particularly. It was a challenging and daunting responsibility. Fortunately the Benson Hotel, under my direction, was already instituting the key control I had essentially demanded before I'd even contemplated attending that 1985 Kansas City conference.

At the Benson, we were slowly installing smoke detectors in every room and had a functioning Emergency Response Team, also under my direction, that could arrive at any point in the thirteen story hotel in approximately three minutes or less.

We were ahead of the game at the historic Benson Hotel, if not leading the way nationally, because of my insistent demands for change. In other words, there were no more hotel room keys with the affixed sticker on a plastic attached sphere reading: "drop in any mailbox," which was typical of how things were done in the old days. When I started at the Benson, room keys for all 287 rooms had been stamped with the room number. In fact the old original brass door knobs on each room still had an O and an H engraved in the center, which stood for the *Oregon Hotel*. That was the original name of the hotel, the *New Oregon Hotel*. This was before the next owner, the millionaire innovator Simon Benson, decided to take over management himself and rename it after himself in 1913.

The front office manager, a stoic woman named Barbara, estimated that over the ten years she had worked there, there were probably over one hundred keys to the most desirable rooms that had *never* been returned at checkout. And the guest room door locks of those rooms had *never* been changed during that time! It was a Connie Francis kind of disaster situation just waiting to happen. I was on top of the key control situation, though, and managing a serious risk as well as I could and quite effectively, I might add. There was simply no other way around such a serious potential risk and I made certain the manager Chet understood that *key control* was of paramount importance.

On the last day of the conference in Kansas, the subject in one seminar changed to a discussion of a million dollar theft of diamonds from the Chicago Westin hotel. I was required to attend this daylong final discussion, and found it to be a fascinating account of a million dollar jewel theft that had been risky and hard to pull off for whoever managed it. I sat in the front row as usual, with approximately twenty five other men, all directors of security from other hotels across the country. The atmosphere was somber as we were given the details of the heist by the panel of three speakers sitting on the stage. There were no films, no slide shows, it was just the men discussing what had happened and bouncing ideas and questions off of each other.

We were told the story of how a hotel guest and diamond salesman had secured his diamonds in a safety deposit box in the secure vault area of the front office of the Westin hotel where he was staying. My ears perked up as I had investigated a 1969 burglary and theft of thousands of dollars in jewelry and gold coins from the H&B Pawn Shop in downtown Portland when I was still a detective with Portland Police Bureau.

The jewelry from that Portland theft was never recovered. And neither was the missing million dollars in diamonds from the Chicago Westin hotel. We were told Lloyds of London, who insured the diamonds, had paid off the claim and the investigation was concluded rather quickly. To me, that seemed odd. Why the hurry?

When the conference was over and I was on the way home on the plane, I kept going over the details of the Chicago theft in my mind. As an experienced investigator nothing about this heist made much sense. The diamonds had been stored in a safety deposit box and locked there *with* a key. Whoever took the diamonds unlocked the deposit box, also with a key. No video cameras were in use. Too convenient, I thought to myself.

There was no camera where common sense would say cameras *should* be located. Things just didn't add up.

This wasn't the 1940s. Surveillance cameras had been in use when my burglary detective coworkers and I had conducted long-term investigations into the crooked pawn shops in Portland accepting fenced goods and that was in the middle 1970s, so why would this Westin Hotel not have video cameras in use in the 80s to keep an eye out for any attempted thefts of such valuable stored items, like diamonds?

From my knowledge of general hotel policy, I knew at least *one* front office person on each of the three shifts, day shift, swing shift and graveyard shift would have to have a key to the safety deposit boxes in the event a guest wished to retrieve their valuables. That would be about four, or perhaps five employees who would have access to both the keys *and* the vault area.

Any experienced investigator could easily interview those employees who would have had the keys *and* access; it would not have been hard to come up with a good idea of who the guilty party likely was. At least this is how I looked at it, because guilty people generally reveal themselves in one way or another.

I knew it was almost impossible for a crook to lie to an experienced investigator, depending on how good they were, or perhaps that was just how I felt about my *own* skills.

I could always spot a liar and in my time in the interview and interrogation rooms at PPB, I rarely failed to get the confession I knew was coming. This required good manners, patience and emotional manipulation—making them think you were their new best friend, using *shame* to get them to confess, and never appearing to judge them, all of which were in my skill set. No threats, no violence just a good strategic plan and follow through.

The fact that Robert A. Bormes, AKA *fast Bobby*, had been the office manager at the time of the Chicago theft jumped out at me, and my detective's radar was pinging hard against my temples. Bormes had had access to both the safety deposit box *and* the vault area. Why had he *not* been the prime suspect, then? Why had he *not* been placed under routine surveillance after the theft? Any detective worth his salt would look closely at the lifestyle of all potential suspects after such a huge theft, to see if they were making any extravagant purchases. But Bormes had never once been a suspect and was in fact promoted and later transferred to the Benson Hotel in Portland.

Lloyds of London paid the claim and the mystery was never solved. The missing million dollars in diamonds was never seen again. Claim paid. Case closed. It was all too easy. Too cut and dried. Something was *rotten in Denmark.*

Of course I was never privy to any investigators notes on the case either from the Chicago police detectives or Lloyds of London, as I was no longer a police detective. But I was certainly witness to the aftermath of the crime. The jewels gone. Claim paid. No suspects. And Fast Bobby who was living high on the hog in Portland only months later. There was a lot to think about with this caper. A lot of planning, thought and preparation had gone into this crime.

The problem is, a million dollars in "hot" diamonds can't just be sold at a pawn shop in another state after being stolen. These jewels *must* have disappeared into the underworld after being spirited out of the country, like so many others before them. I *knew* the Chicago Westin Hotel diamonds probably had left the country on a jet, as that is often how it's done. I knew this from what I'd learned about jewelry heists working as a police detective in the Burglary Detail with PPB.

The possibility of collusion also occurred to me. Say the jewelry salesman was in on the planning. We'll call him Skip. Skip places the diamonds in the safety deposit box. Then he has his accomplice in the hotel "steal" them. It is a mystery. The diamonds "just disappeared" and no one saw or heard a thing. No one is prosecuted and the claim is paid. Now Skip and their crook friends have a million in cash and they still have the diamonds.

I also considered the location of the diamond heist—Chicago, the traditional home of many gangsters who would be more than willing to pull off a caper this daring and complex. A thought kept repeating in my mind. *Bormes should have been a prime suspect from the get-go. Instead he was promoted and transferred out of state.*

In my time as a street cop and police detective I knew of several corrupt men who committed crimes of various sorts, and then were promoted and transferred to different departments later, instead of being fired. This pattern spared certain individuals embarrassment and it was timeless in its predictability. The Chicago jewel caper reminded me of this longstanding tradition of protecting dirty crooks and then transferring them, to spare an establishment or an individual embarrassment.

This pattern has also been proven to have occurred in the American Catholic Church, as well. Protect predator priests, promote or transfer them out, and whatever happens, happens. Keep the chaos moving along just as long as its not happening in *your* backyard.

Was the fact that Fast Bobby was transferred out of town also a part of the conspiracy? Was he offered a new life and job in a new town with enough money to live large? And why did his wife keep returning to Chicago? Was she the *Bag Man* in this scenario? There were a lot of questions I would never have the answers to. The only thing I knew for sure was that the investigation into this million dollar theft was either done by amateurs or co-conspirators. No one wanted the truth, just apparently the cash.

When I returned to work at the Benson Hotel after the conference, I shared all the information with Chet about the necessary changes in the way hotels were currently doing business, showing him a few printed articles and lists of various concerns we needed to think about that I'd received at the conference.

There was a lot of information on how we would have to comply with corporate policy by upgrading the Benson to current standards. I explained the well-known aftermath in detail regarding the Connie Francis rape case verdict. Chet seemed never to have heard of the Connie Francis case, which didn't surprise me. I explained to him that we would continue with guest room key control, fire safety and the importance of regularly patrolling the hallways and common areas to insure guest safety and that meant adding to my staff of security officers.

I informed Chet that our newly installed cameras would be increased by two, so that I could monitor the Vault area, where the guest safety deposit boxes were located. By now Chet was resigned to the fact that changes were in effect that he could not put off. And I knew he was worried his father would be looking over his shoulder if my mandated changes were stalled by *his* hesitancy to sign purchase orders and follow my suggestions.

At no time did I mention my suspicions to Chet that a jewel thief with a lot of connections to Chicago was now working at the Benson Hotel. I kept that to myself. Chet was easily frightened and I figured what he didn't know couldn't hurt him. So, did Fast Bobby Bormes actually get away scot free with the theft of a million dollars in diamonds? It appears that he did, in my seasoned opinion, and I will *always* believe that.

****

The other Jewel thief who got away scot free after a big caper was William Wells Lewis. Before Billy went to prison for the Zoo burglary in July of 1969, I believe he ripped off Lou Tobin's H&B pawn shop on SW Third Avenue in downtown Portland the month before, in June 1969.

This is how I know the burglar was Billy Lewis: Lou Tobin came to work one morning in June of 1969 and unlocked the front door to the pawn shop. Inside, the store was a-shambles with counters and office furniture pushed out of the way and knocked over to get a clear working area in front of the safe. The safe, a tall double door, reach-in vault, had a vibration alarm attached so if the safe was moved or struck with a hammer the alarm would go off.

The safe however was visibly empty.

The many small drawers inside the safe were pulled out and emptied and the pigeon holes cleaned out. The office front door was unlocked by the burglar and relocked when he left. The alarm to the safe was turned off with a key. Only a safe cracker as skilled as Billy Lewis was capable of making the correct keys. When I showed Lou Tobin several photos of Billy Lewis, he recognized Lewis immediately, saying: "That's the guy who was hanging around in the front a few days ago and looking in the windows at the jewelry displays!"

I suspected Billy had another person, possibly his wife, looking around inside the store, pretending to be an interested customer. Her role was to block the view of the front door while Billy inserted a blank key into the door lock and wiggled it around, back and forth, for those precious faint impressions that would help him create the key, later on.

That day in 1969, Lou Tobin was in severe distress as he viewed the disaster that was his pawn shop. He was ranting, and raving and nearly hyperventilating. "How could this possibly happen?!" he demanded, while mopping his forehead with a white initialed handkerchief. He was a tall man about six foot three and slender. His grey hair was thin with curly fringes and his body straight up and down like a board. His shoulders were bony, too, what he had of them.

Lou always looked like he needed a good meal and as I stood there, I realized I'd never seen him so much as sip from a cup of coffee before. Other pawn shop owners were more relaxed, sometimes eating a sandwich during one of my visits and always with hot coffee nearby in a comforting large mug and always enough to offer me a cup, which I generally refused.

Lou looked a little green in the face like he was ready to vomit or cry, or both. Not only was all the jewelry and gold gone, he realized hundreds of people holding pawn tickets would be returning to the H & B to reclaim their items, and what could he tell them? Technically the missing jewelry was the property of the ticket holder to be redeemed at a later date. Lou would have a lot of explaining to do when irate customers returned to reclaim their precious could-never-be-replaced family heirloom piece. I encouraged him to calm down, as he paced the store, wringing his hands, sweating, and breathing heavily while declaring his life was over.

I was able to calculate an approximate sum of money stolen, by going through the pawn tickets to determine what was missing. I knew Tobin loaned between eight and ten percent of the retail value of the pawned item. I calculated the loss at well over $100,000. Some of the stolen items were distinctive pieces of rare antique women's jewelry, but a lot of the jewelry was of lesser value and was referred to in the business as "breakers."

Breakers were usually older pieces of jewelry from the 1920s, the teens or the turn of the century that were of little value, like old style costume jewelry that Flapper Girls wore during the the Roaring Twenties. While the diamonds, if there were any, were almost always an "old mine cut" they were still valuable but the piece itself was out of style and unpopular.

Consider that a Grandma died and her family sold all her old jewelry which then winds up in your local pawnshop. Out of style jewelry was generally broken up and the good parts harvested, so to speak. The diamonds were removed and the gold melted down. Then there was the difference between an old mine cut diamond, and a modern brilliant cut diamond. The difference is this: old mine cut diamonds have a smaller top but are larger near the bottom, in essence there is more diamond there. Brilliant cut diamonds have a broader top, but the bottom is shallow and there is less diamond present in the cut.

I had a long history with Lou Tobin, spanning several years. As a burglary detective I was often in daily contact with the pawnshops looking through their loan tickets for a match to the lists of stolen items I was looking for to return to the good Portland citizens who'd been burglarized or robbed. Over the years I found Lou to be dishonest, and evasive. Burglars I interrogated sometimes told me they regularly sold their loot to "Tobin over at the H&B." When I would check out their story I often found Tobin had no written record of the items the burglars told me they had sold to him. They had no reason to lie, but Tobin did.

Yes, in my seasoned opinion, Billy Lewis had dealt Lou Tobin a devastating blow. He must have known that Tobin was crooked and figured he had a burglary coming. But in this case the evidence was slim. I almost felt sorry for Tobin—almost.

I remember an occasion, right around the time I was promoted to detective in 1967, when I was checking the tickets at the H&B and I saw some of the very jewelry in a display case that I knew for certain was stolen in another burglary case I had just begun investigating. The owner had included a photo of her lost piece of jewelry. It was an old fashioned 1920s era gold brooch with a 1.5 carat, old-mine-cut center diamond, surrounded by several small diamonds and set in genuine gold filigree.

It was a distinct piece, and I had a photograph of it and it was now for sale in Tobin's display case! I stood there looking down into the glass case in mild disbelief. There it was! Finally, after a moment I showed the stolen report to him and the photograph of the broach, which I had with me in my briefcase. I pointed, deadpan, to the broach in his display case and told him he needed to hand it over to me so I could return it to its rightful owner.

But Lou seemed troubled, he shuffled his feet around, stood sideways and avoided eye contact with me and after trying to play dumb he refused to give me the jewelry, shaking his head no. He started breathing hard and it seemed as if he was about to throw a hissy fit, as I could see he was becoming more agitated. He complained that he had bought it and "paid good money for it" and he intended to keep it. He was very sorry, he said but he didn't know that it was stolen when he bought it, and he explained that because of that, it was *his* possession and he did *not* have to surrender it.

I listened patiently, waiting for Lou to finish. Now, it was my turn to explain to Mr. Tobin, something he already knew. What I explained to him was that it was a hazard of the business he was in that he may occasionally, even inadvertently buy jewelry which had been stolen. I also explained that "the title to stolen merchandise can never be transferred to another person." Case in point, I told him: "If you stole the Mona Lisa and took the painting home, it would still not be yours. Just because you bought the jewelry in good faith, Lou, is irrelevant. If you knew it was stolen or not, it is still *not* your possession."

As I was explaining this to him, I further told him that now that he knew it was stolen then he must surrender it to me, and that it was my job as a Portland burglary detective to recover merchandise which had been reported as stolen and which I could *prove* had been stolen. Furthermore, now that I was looking at the stolen merchandise in the glass case, I was duty-bound to return it to the owner, whether he approved or not.

Lou stood there shaking his head no, and still refused to hand over the broach. He was testing me. Next I offered Tobin two solutions: "Look Lou, we can do this the easy way or the hard way," I told him patiently. "You can either give me the stolen broach right now or I can just as easily station a uniformed police officer at the door. He'll keep an eye on the case, and make sure the broach remains safe, and in the exact location without any interference from you. Then I can return to the station where I'll draw up the paperwork for a search warrant, *and* I'll get it back *that* way. It's up to you. What do you think passersby will think with a patrolman stationed at your door?"

Lou stood there silently, still testing me, looking down at his scuffed Wing Tip dress shoes. Finally, I explained I could easily find a judge who would gladly sign such a valid search warrant. I told Tobin that the whole process could possibly take two, maybe three hours tops and that either way, I was going to get that antique brooch back to the old lady who had had it stolen from her home in the West Hills, whether he liked it or not.

Lou's shoulders slouched even more than usual and his face twisted into a sneer as he realized he had been defeated and distinctly out played. He reached into his pants pocket for the key, and then unlocked the display case. He sullenly retrieved the glittering broach and placed it into a small brown envelope. Still he would not look at me as he pushed the envelope toward me across the glass countertop in silent, reproachful disgust.

Then without another word or glance in my direction, he turned his back on me, shuffled his stooped shoulders toward the back of the shop and into his private office, sitting down dejectedly in a chair near the door.

This interaction was typical of my dealings with Lou Tobin over the years. On more than one occasion I sent a report on his nefarious activities to the city license bureau to re-evaluate whether he should be allowed to do business in the city as a pawn shop operator. I heard they sent the H&B warning letters, but nothing ever changed with Lou. He did what he wanted and seemed to feel he was above the law.

I mention Lou Tobin's attitude only because the two other pawn shops on SW 3rd Avenue operated in stark contrast. Two doors south from the H&B was a pawn shop owned by Milt Arnstein. Milt was in his middle sixties, was bald with a little grey fringe, and a chubby middle. He had a big smile above his double chin, and always had a cooperative attitude. Milt smiled good naturedly whenever I showed up with my lists of stolen property. He never argued when he had to give up property I found to be stolen. Milt always looked well fed and never tried to lie to me. Perhaps that was the difference between him and the rail thin Lou Tobin. Milt just seemed like a happier person.

An old German man named Otto ran the third pawn shop on Third Street. Otto was short and had to step up on a stool when anyone came in the door so he could look them in the eye during transactions. He was friendly to everyone but kept a loaded .38 snub nose in plain view on top of the safe behind the counter, sending a clear message to any would-be robbers not to mess with him. No one ever argued with Otto and he never argued with me when it came time to give up a stolen piece he had inadvertently purchased. Otto and Milt seemed honest and never wasted my time by lying or bickering with me. Lou Tobin was their opposite and that's one of the reasons I never trusted him or had any sympathy for him. Lou knew at least half of what he bought was hot merchandise and he didn't care. All he cared about was the money he could get for the items.

****

Billy Lewis, in my opinion, got away scot free with the H&B pawn shop burglary. I am convinced of it and convinced that only *he* could have done it, because no other boxman was as slick as Billy. It was a brilliantly planned and beautifully executed caper, and had to have been a greatly rewarding heist for Billy and whoever else was involved. We heard through the grapevine, through one of our informants, that the $100,000 plus in jewelry and gold from the H&B wound up on a plane to Singapore via Honolulu within 24 hours of the job.

Of course Billy never talked about his other crimes, and as he was headed to the Oregon State Penitentiary for ten years for the Zoo burglary anyway, he remained consistently silent during any questioning by anyone, including me. In my mind I reconciled Billy getting away with the H&B pawn shop burglary, by realizing that one crooked crook had ripped off another, as they so often do. And in the end, they both got their karma.

Justice is not always achieved via the judicial system, though. I think there was *legal justice* which Billy Lewis received and then there was *moral justice* which Lou Tobin received.

So the score wound up being this: Chubby Charlie Wright, the not so dashing jewel thief went to prison for interstate transportation of $17,000 in diamonds which he stole from a Lloyd Center jewelry store. Charlie was caught red handed and didn't get away with it, and I got a commendation from the FBI for solving the crime and for the $17,000 in diamonds being returned.

William Wells Lewis, a very ordinary looking jewel thief certainly did get away scot free with the H&B caper, and the notorious ripping off of Lou Tobin. There is no way this can be proven in a traditional investigative sense but I *know* who did that caper. I also know the prison cell Billy occupied in Salem Oregon didn't much care which crime he was locked up for. He had been outsmarted by a longshoreman eating a ham and cheese sandwich and some pretty good follow up police work by two engaged detectives—me and John Wayne Wesson.

Fast Bobby Bormes, also something less than a dashing figure, if not a pitiable one, certainly did get away scot free with the theft of one million dollars in diamonds from the Chicago Westin Hotel where he was the office manager. While again there is no way to prove his involvement, in my seasoned opinion, I will always believe that Bormes *was* the man who got away with that caper.

Final note: about a year after I left the Benson Hotel around 1986 for more lucrative work as a security consultant in hotel

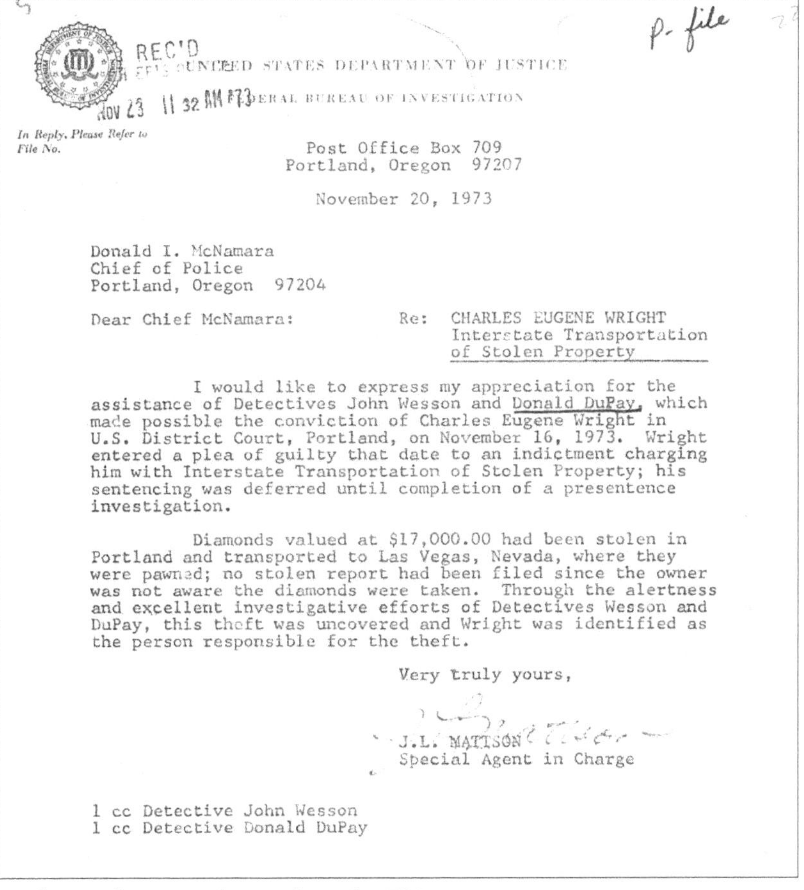

My letter of commendation from the FBI.

and parking lot lawsuit cases, wherein I testified in court on a regular basis as an expert witness, I returned one afternoon to the Benson and had coffee with two of the security officer's still working for the Benson, whom I had hired previously. We had always been friendly and had stayed in touch.

One was a woman named Norma, a motherly type and extremely efficient security officer. She was a middle-aged woman who could shame a drunk bar patron better than any other security officer in my employ. She could stop them from swearing in an instant, and then have them marching to their room with just a stern look over the top of her granny glasses.

The other officer was a thirty-five-year old Hispanic man named Victor Quinones. He was tall, muscular, had a pencil thin mustache, smooth olive skin and jet black hair, perfectly slicked back and well trimmed. Victor was incredibly good looking and when his charming smile didn't work on a drunken patron; his stern face did the job, instead. Women patrons never argued with Victor. His smile melted them, and men were smart enough to do as he instructed. Both of these officers were assets to the Benson hotel, and I was proud to have hired them.

As we sat and talked about old times, and after most of the small talk was over with, they both leaned forward and I got the lowdown on all the hotel gossip that had happened after I'd left. This included details on which bellman was flirting with which room attendant and which cooks had still survived well enough to continue working for Xavier, who was as ever still the abusive tyrant he had always been, and what employees had been fired for stealing food or wine from the kitchen and other forms of mundane gossip.

Finally, Victor and Norma got to what I was most interested in hearing about—Fast Bobby Bormes! "Mr. Bormes," according to Victor and Norma, was assigned as a Weekend Duty Officer; a hotel policy in which different department heads took turns being in charge on the weekends. They were expected to walk through the halls, check the kitchens and the restaurants and inspect the quality of the room service by the maids. This meant enjoying all the perks, which included staying in the best suites, and having free room service of course, which meant all meals free of charge.

The front office manager, Janet, on one occasion several months after I'd left to work as a consultant, was tasked with talking with Bormes who had been assigned as the Weekend Duty Officer. After coming on and pleasantly chatting with several other employees, about an hour or so later, suddenly Bormes could not be found. He was not answering his radio and my former security officers became alarmed and went out looking for him. Finding his room, they knocked but received no reply. Finally, they unlocked the door and discreetly pushed the door open to quite a surprise.

Norma and Victor told me, both with amused looks on their faces, that they found Bormes passed out, nearly face down in a scattered pile of cocaine. His oily nose and unwashed face was covered in the white powder, his mouth was hanging open and his drooling tongue flopped out of his mouth. Bormes was unconscious and half sitting on the edge of a wooden chair, while also slumped over a desk. His arms were loose on the table and his face literally encased in the powdery pile of cocaine. And he was snoring. I was somehow not surprised as they told me their tale of woe and we all chuckled, shaking our heads.

Learning that Bormes was a cokehead put it all in perspective for me. All the puzzle pieces came together, and as a former detective, I relished knowing my instincts about Bormes had been spot on from the get-go. It was probably the need for cocaine that prompted the Chicago diamond heist in the first place. Victor told me he and Norma didn't call the police. It would have been horrible publicity for the hotel and they didn't want it. It was the same old story. Do damage control and send the silent offender on his way.

So, Bormes again was not arrested for his bad behavior, but he was quietly terminated by the management after a humiliating meeting detailing what Victor and Norma discovered. I can only imagine Bormes and his intense embarrassment having to be terminated like that and having to listen to Victor and Norma explain to Chet what they had seen. Bormes no longer worked for Portland's finest hotel and they further told me that he moved out of his expensive apartment, because he could no longer afford the rent, and of course that meant, he left town soon after being fired by Chet as well.

Despite both Billy Lewis and Fast Bobby Bormes getting away scot-free with two very daring heists, they also suffered for their crimes in other ways, too, though it took some time for those repercussions to finally take place in their lives.

****

Conclusion: Safe burglars, the really good "safe mechanics" or "box men" like Billy Lewis are a lost breed and their time has passed. That time in American crime history will never return. Box men of that era have been defeated essentially by the modern technology of a postmodern world. Alarms are more sophisticated today with infrared sensors and motion detectors and pressure sensitive alarms which go off if a diamond is removed from a display case, or if someone even breathes too close to the alarm. Technology even allows store alarms to be armed and disarmed by remote control over a smartphone like an IPhone, so there is no door lock to jiggle, try and pick, or create a key for via the lost art of key impressions, which truly was an art form in its heyday, by those who could do it, men like Billy Lewis.

Today's jewel thieves walk into a jewelry store with a shotgun and take what they want. Or they steal after being hired to work there, but even that is rarer these days due to surveillance cameras. No need to worry about prying things open and sweating over an old safe with a torch because they just aren't around anymore. Other than as attractive oddities in historical societies and museums, old safes are a thing of the past.

Even in the days of safe burglaries, there were other ways a person could steal diamonds or jewelry. A well dressed person might enter a jewelry store, looking like they could afford to be there. They would engage the clerk, looking at several diamond rings or loose diamonds, and after picking the most expensive one, bolt out the door into a waiting car never to be seen again. And neither was the jewelry, or the stones.

Or they would manage to swallow a diamond surreptitiously and then claim innocence when the diamond couldn't be located, as in the classic 1978 film *King of the Gypsies*, starring Eric Roberts. Either way, the days of the jewel thieves who were active in the 1960s and 1970s, when I was a detective are long gone and will never return.

Being that safe burglary could be a complex crime, or a matter of simply tearing open a safe, I had mixed feelings about the box men who made these crimes their work. I never respected

Fast Bobby Bormes or Charlie Wright, they were too repulsive in multiple ways for me to admire. And they were also stupid crooks who didn't care who they hurt, so I felt nothing but contempt for them.

The only "box man" I ever managed to admire was in fact Billy Lewis. He was an interesting person, quiet, and aware that he didn't have to talk or give up information. He was never arrogant, but had a strange humble quality about him that aided him in being a good criminal. He was extremely skilled as a locksmith, and was an expert with a cutting torch. And he the only box man I knew of who could create a key by making impressions.

Lewis was far more intelligent than your average safe burglar and I had to admire the patient planning that went into the H&B heist and the Zoo burglary. Despite this odd feeling of admiration, I didn't feel sorry for him when he was arrested. I was glad he got ten years, this for a man with no previous criminal record. It is possible he was allowed out earlier; though I never kept track of him after his 1969 arrest to find out, and don't know how his prison sentence went down.

Years later I became acquainted with a woman named Patty Katz, Aka "Peppermint Patty." She had worked with Billy Lewis at the White Elephant night club. She was only 21 in 1968, which would have been the year before Billy did the zoo burglary, and Billy would have been in his forties. Patty shared her memories with me and my wife Theresa, about that special time in her life:

"There I was, young, dumb and wide-eyed. I was working as

a cocktail waitress, and began my new job only two days after my twenty-first birthday. I grew to know and love the night-life and I learned to boogie!" There were two separate crowds that came into the White Elephant in Beaverton.

The "day shift" or "cocktail hour" crowd, and then there was the rock and roll crowd at night. I was part of the night shift. The club would fill with young people and the fun would begin for me. Sometimes I would come in early to have dinner before my shift. I would sit in the bar and listen to all "those old guys" chatting about what I thought was "old-people stuff."

Then one day I went to work and there was a new 'old guy' and it was like he was holding court. He was talking and everyone was listening or asking questions. He had an audience. Then I heard someone ask: "Well how was prison?" And I thought, "Who is this guy? Prison? There's a prisoner in my bar?"

So, very bravely, I went behind the bar, pretending I was putting my tray together. I turned around and asked him: "You seem like a well known guy, I'm Peppermint Patty, but who are you?" He told me a little bit about himself. Then later, I asked: "Why were you in prison AND are you here to hurt someone?"

That was my first day of knowing Billy Lewis! He was the new bartender. Well, Billy became sort of a hero to me. Those were the days! If we didn't put our tips in the bank; it didn't seem to count as taxable money, so I filled up shoeboxes with my tip money and then had "disposable money." I was very naive and pretty green. Billy became my "financial advisor" and suggested I invest in jewelry.

I was young, dumb and green behind the ears. I didn't have

enough money "to buy big" as Billy called it, but I was able to buy a few pieces from him that were fairly valuable. First a necklace and then I would save up to buy a ring, that's how it started. I really wasn't a very big investor, so Billy sent me to a pawn-shop in lower south-west Portland.

Every so often I would buy another piece to add to my "jewel collection" as I called it. There was only one person I would buy from, other than Billy. I wish I could remember his name, but I've forgotten. I always told people where I got my stuff, and I gave them a special card I got from the Pawn Shop dealer, who had given me quite a number of unique pieces. If my friends presented the card, I would get a little kick-back or dollars off my next purchase at the pawn shop. It worked out.

Once I asked Billy, how come I was such a special customer and he said: "Well kid, you wear the pieces to work and people notice, then they ask you: 'where did you get that?' You tell them, and they go to your connection and our business grows a little bit."

So I guess I was a very small part of the Great Billy Lewis story. Another day I went to work early and there was a new guy standing behind the bar. He and Billy had been "roommates" down in Salem. His name was Bill, and he was old and grumpy! (Both of those really "old guys" were only in their late thirties or forties) Every time I went to work a little bit early, I would get to meet a few more gangsters. I remember Billy didn't like rock music, saying: "You call that loud fucking noise, music?!" Each time he would say that, I'd say, "G-pa, you'd better have another Cutty Sark! The "G" and "pa" meant gangster and Grandpa, the Cutty Sark was his favorite Scotch.

I can't remember all of the folks I met, but each time I relieved Billy from his shift, I got to see some of the folks sitting at the bar, swapping stories with each other about some of the "great gangsters" in my work life that we all came across. Knowing Billy Lewis was a great adventure for a young woman, so very green in the world."

Patty Katz, (a lovely woman who was cherished by her many friends and family) has since passed on. She provided a lively and realistic perspective of what it was like to be a part of that subculture during the late 60s and early 70s. So, when you think of a jewel thief, and you think of some debonair Cary Grant type in a well-tailored suit oozing coolness from every pore, understand that is not generally the reality. Most jewel thieves are the last person you would ever expect would be capable of stealing jewelry or the contents of a safe during a high stakes burglary. Rather, they are the "normal looking" people we see all around us, and it is their very average demeanor and appearance that help them blend into the crowd so effectively and deceive people.

You have to wonder at times if crime *does* pay. It seems that it did to those crooks who chose that dangerous lifestyle. When we saw all those luxury cars parked around well-known gangster hangouts like Bill's Gold Coin or the Rimrock on Columbia Boulevard, or of course at the White Elephant in Beaverton or any number of past gangster hangouts, including the notorious Mural Room on SW Jefferson Street, it would seem that crime *did* pay.

What most people see is the temporary flash, the toys—the fancy cars, the nice threads—the glittering jewelry and of course the pretty women on the arms of the men who were those crooks. To those of us who endeavored to keep society safe from many of these predators we saw the other side of the lifestyle. We saw the defeated wives and vacant-eyed children visiting husbands and fathers in prison.

We saw the hands of those men within the penitentiary walls sticking through prison bars. Those hands were mostly working class hands, with dirty fingernails and calloused palms from hard blue collar work. We saw the defeated faces of the men who knew they were looking at ten years or longer helpless within the confines of prison life. We saw the ultimate end of the fast life, the stark reality of criminals caught, with nowhere to go but back inside a tiny prison cell to wait, to remember and to regret how they allowed their lives to go sideways.

CHAPTER 2

THE TROUBLED AND DISTRESSED WOMEN OF ALBINA

"From 30 feet away she looked like a lot of class. From 10 feet away she looked like something made up to be seen from 30 feet away."

—Raymond Chandler, author of *The High Window*

Life puts a hard edge on people and no one knows this better than a cop. There are predators and there are victims. That part of crime never changes. This section of the book details some of the women I can remember, women whose faces and stories remain vivid in my memory and whose lives I still recall. Most of the women I came across were victims of all sorts of chaos, unhappiness and bad luck and generally doing the best they could.

In my seventeen year career in law enforcement I saw a lot of victims. They were a part of my every working day spanning six years as a street cop working the Albina ghetto, and eleven more years working as a police detective. I worked Burglary and Homicide, among other details which included the Safe Detail, Morals and even Check Fraud, and in all that time, it was never an easy profession, particularly when dealing with troubled women who were in distress.

Their struggles ranged from spousal abuse, drug trafficking, tragic car accidents, housefires, burglaries, robberies, forcible rape and the sexual molestation of their children. Some women I saw only after their deaths, as they were the victims of horrible acts of vicious murder. I even came across the peripheral victims of auto-erotic asphyxia. (AEA) is a form of masturbation that involves mild oxygen deprivation but it often goes wrong and turns fatal for the practitioner. Most of the deaths involving (AEA) were young men, but they *all* had fathers, siblings *and* mothers who were left behind, bewildered and wondering what the Hell had happened.

Then there were the numerous women who were left to deal with the new reality of a loved one who died in bed of a sudden heart attack. Or committed suicide by shooting themselves in the head, breathing exhaust fumes, locked in a garage or they hanged themselves from the bathroom showerhead with a telephone cord. Survivors of these tragedies are left to deal with the aftermath, they are generally alone and more often than not, they are women.

The nurturers, the mothers and sisters of us all are the saddest of crime victims, in my opinion. Yet, I also remember some evil women, those who committed crimes like burglary, assault with a gun or a knife or even a spiked high heeled shoe. Though they could often appear completely evil and toxic, I knew they were miserable, too. The forgers, drunks, abusive mothers and street hookers were often so hardened they could assault a grown man, knock him down and run off with his wallet without a second glance or even a perfunctory chuckle at his expense.

What I remember most about my first encounter with a woman in my official capacity as a newly recruited Portland Police officer was how hard she hit me with her stiletto heel, *and* how she smelled. It was my first week on the job and I was a green rookie working with Paul "Pete" Peterson, a seasoned officer who acted as my coach in our district, which was North Portland. It was nearly eleven thirty at night when we pulled through the parking lot of the Nite Hawk Café and Lounge located on North Interstate and Portland Blvd, which has now been renamed *Rosa Parks Way*.

Driving slowly through the lot we noticed a small blond boy about four-years-old, alone, and crying hysterically in the back seat of a parked car. I remember the weather was chilly, and the boy was underdressed in what looked like scruffy pale colored clothing. Pete, as my coach liked to be called, pulled into the parking lot at the far west end, halted our police car and jumped out.

He retrieved the youngster from the back seat, opening the door and gently gathering him up in his arms, and out of the unlocked car. He held him for a moment, cradling him and letting his head loll on his shoulder as the boy wept brokenly, talking quietly to him, telling him everything would be okay. After a moment, Pete handed the small boy to me. He told me to hold him, and that he was going to "go in and find the mother!" The way he said *mother* sounded more like a curse word.

I held the boy, though not nearly as expertly as Pete had, walked back to the car, and maneuvered a blanket from out of the back seat. I snuggled the blanket around his shoulders and under him, and placed him in the back seat of our car. "Everything's gonna be alright now," I said quietly.

When the boy stopped crying for a moment, I asked where his mother was. He pointed his little index finger in the direction of the lounge which was at that time located in the front of the building. "In der!" he said brokenly and then, upon remembering where his mother was, he began wailing again.

By now Pete had already stormed through the door of the lounge filled with righteous indignation. Pete was a husband and father to four children, and had no patience for unfit parents who were "selfish" as he put it and didn't take care of their kids properly. Upon entering the restaurant, after he had flung the door open, he stood there at the threshold, peering into the darkened room. I was placing the boy in the backseat, while my eyes were still tracking Pete and I could tell he was angry.

About five minutes later, Pete reappeared, walking out the front entrance with a woman, pulling her aggressively by the arm. When the little boy saw his mother, he reached out with both arms beseechingly. "Mama!" he cried over and over. She glanced over at the boy, dismissively and ignored him.

"What are ya doin' drinkin' in a bar while your son is out here ALONE?!" Pete demanded with contempt dripping from his voice as he dragged her into the parking lot.

"I was doin' just fine until *you* came in and jerked me off the stool!" the woman sneered in response.

"*YOU* are under arrest for being drunk in a public place *and* for child endangerment! Turn around!"After Pete informed the woman she was under arrest for being drunk in a public place and abandoning her child—the fight was on!

The woman stood about five foot five, was in her early forties and pretty in a cheap sort of way with short bleached blond hair and too much makeup. She was wearing a tight white knit skirt and a red pullover Cashmere sweater. As she started to wiggle and squirm trying to get out of Pete's grasp, she was able to reach down and get one high heeled shoe off and that's when she turned aggressive, and began hitting both of us with the sharp spiked heel. For a small woman, she could hit hard and she was strong and quick.

She pounded me on my arms and shoulders several times, and was trying to strike me in the face and on my head, her eyes wild with drunken rage. She was cussing a blue streak and I kept turning my head and dancing around her, trying to grab her arms and dodging her to avoid the blows. The strong smell of whisky was on her breath and she fairly reeked of booze as if she had been drinking all day.

I remember the smell was overpowering and blended with the fragrance of a nice department store perfume she was wearing. It was a chaotic experience and confusing for me as a new police recruit. I'd never experienced anything like it before. She was a woman and all my life I had been taught by my father *never* to hit a woman. I had never witnessed violence between a man and woman, as my parents never fought and I was simply inexperienced.

Pete, who was a veteran cop in his late forties, quickly grew tired of struggling with the woman. The look on his face told me he was fed up and was going to end it. He showed me exactly what to do. He backed up and stood for a moment, with a disgusted look on his face and then—BAM! He hit her on the left side of her jaw with a wide swinging forearm, knocking her backwards and stunning her. *I was amazed.* Pete was totally in charge. As she was stunned and stumbling around, yet still on her feet, we were able to grab her, turn her around, handcuff her and sit her on the ground, telling her to stay put.

"You stay right there and don't you MOVE! You got that? Or I'll put on the leg irons!" Pete said disgustedly.

Pete went to the car, picked up the microphone, took a deep breath and lit a cigarette at the same time he was getting dispatch on the line. He asked for the *Women's Protective Division*, (WPD) to come and take charge of the boy. And to, "bring Number 99" our reliable and *only* paddy wagon PPB had at the time. Old 99 would come and pick up our female prisoner and take her to jail. Pete also told dispatch to bring along "Number 95" which was the tow truck, to come and tow her car. I learned a valuable lesson from my training partner that night. Male or female, if you attack a cop with a sharp stiletto heel, or any other part of your body, and if you resist arrest, you might just get your ass kicked in the form of a solid forearm to the jaw.

* * * *

Another memorable interaction I had with a Portland woman was so intense and dangerous that I remember her full name: Alice Marie Johnson. I even remember her address. But most of all I remember her face and the expressions of defiance, anger, submission, and finally defeat that passed over her features during my short interaction with her.

I remember the smears of blood on her dirty pale colored dress—it might have been pink but it might have been yellow, too. I can't recall exactly, being that this was sixty years ago. I remember the smears of blood on her face and hands as I watched her wipe her sweaty forehead with the back of her hand, the bloody straight razor still clutched tightly in her hand.

I was working "first night" which is the four to midnight shift out of East Precinct with Officer Kenny Zapp when we were called to a North Mississippi street address by a Radio Cab driver. He had been hijacked by a black woman with a straight razor whom he had run across at the Emanuel Hospital. Dispatch informed us that *Miss Alice Johnson* had slashed her boyfriend "Napoleon" at their residence. The boyfriend escaped to Emanuel Hospital, seeking medical attention, but Johnson followed him with the intent to do him even more bodily harm.

After arriving at the hospital either on foot or by bus, Johnson ran past doctors and nurses, and then slashed a white security guard who was trying to protect Napoleon as he was waiting to get stitches from a physician. The assault on the security guard resulted in a severed tendon in the guard's right wrist and a lot of lost blood—a very serious offense which would come with a long prison sentence for Alice.

After Johnson failed to harm her boyfriend, slashing the security guard instead, she panicked and ran out the front door of the ER room, and jumped into a cab which was idling by the curb near the ER exit. She waved the bloody straight razor menacingly at the cab driver, also a white man, and ordered him to drive her home, obviously not the smartest thing to do. Terrified, the cab driver drove Alice to her house, after she gave the man her full address–another not so smart thing.

The house was located nearby at 3540 North Mississippi. Upon arrival, Alice jumped out and ran up the front stairs. She rushed into the unlocked house, locking the door behind her and hid. When we got to the call, outside the house, the driver was waiting for us, still shaken, out of breath, and pointing up the concrete stairs in disbelief. Alice had made the task of finding her much easier than most criminals would have.

"I thought she was gonna kill me!"

"You'll be alright, you're unhurt," I told him calmly.

"I can't believe she actually gave me her address! What a dummy!"

"Okay, you just wait here."

The man assured us that Johnson was indeed still in the house although there were no lights on. As we looked up at the darkened windows, the cab driver complained that he had not been paid. I told him to wait as my partner and I jogged up the concrete stairs to secure the house, and mentioned over my shoulder that he probably *wouldn't* get paid either and should just be satisfied that he was still alive and hadn't been slashed like the two other men. When he continued to argue with me, I told him: "Shut your mouth!"

I knocked on the door for a couple of minutes shouting "Police! Open the door!" After several minutes of being ignored I put a foot to the middle of the front door and easily kicked it open. The door was flimsy thin wood and cracked open with no trouble. It was totally dark inside and quiet. I shouted several times "Alice! We're police officers! Come out!" while shining my flashlight here and there and looking around.

Alice was hiding quietly somewhere in the darkened house with her straight razor, probably thinking she might get away with two felony assaults with a deadly weapon if she was not found. But I was intent on finding her, and I couldn't help but chuckle thinking she'd hijacked a cab driver, and then ordered him to take her directly to her home after giving him the home address.

After I walked into the house, I remember the hair standing up on the back of my neck. As I was walking around, I realized she could jump out of the darkness and slash me at any moment. The interior of the house was totally dark. Kenny and I stayed side by side both using our flashlights to silently search the two bedroom home.

When we tried to switch on a light, we realized the house had no electricity. It was a shambles of course, showing the violent struggle between Alice and Napoleon, her boyfriend, which had occurred less than an hour before. The house was filled with rundown furniture, there were no curtains on the windows and dirt, grit and small bits of dried leaves covered the upswept floor of the living room, with a smattering of peanut shells scattered around, too. On an end table in a far corner of the room we saw a small votive candle that was almost spent, still flickering and casting a meager yellow light.

In the bedroom, there were some blood splatters on the dirty bed linen. The bed consisted of a mattress and box spring on the floor. In the kitchen a couple of ratty parlor chairs were turned over and some dirty pots and pans had been thrown on the floor. There was a sink full of stinking dishes and rotting food, which made the kitchen smell like a chicken coop.

It was a rundown home already but the scuffle and general disarray in each room made the house even more dismal and surreal, like some kind of bizarre nightmare scene in a Fellini art film. This was a home infected with the chaos of grinding poverty, general ignorance and the hopelessness of dysfunction and despair.

I could see Alice was not hiding on the main floor and there was no attic, or second floor to search. From the kitchen we found the entrance to the basement, and again I began shouting for Johnson to show herself. It was eerily quiet and the darkness seemed so thick our flashlights had trouble cutting through it. I tightened my grip on my service revolver and could hear the firing range officer's voice in my head warning me: "Always make the *first* shot count, DuPay!"

I was hyper-aware as I started down the stairs, a common reaction when your body is loaded with adrenalin and you're sweating bullets. The silence was deafening; it rumbled through my brain and made me wary and vigilant. I could hear the thin squeak of my heavy leather gun belt as I barely moved—listening intently. There were about ten stairs down to the concrete basement floor and the prospect of going down into that deep darkness was not something I relished. I wanted the night to be over. I was exhausted already and hadn't eaten in hours, a common issue among police officers—finding the time to eat between calls. My stomach was rumbling and I could feel myself fading. I needed a cheeseburger and two or three cups of hot coffee.

Our flashlights slashed through the darkness but I could see only the floor, and nothing else, as there didn't appear to be any basement windows. I stepped on the fourth step down, and the stair tread squeaked and I froze again, holding my breath. I hoped the old step could hold my weight of 190 pounds. It seemed my senses were acute enough to hear breathing and even my own heart beating. I concentrated for a moment making sure it was not my breathing I was hearing. I looked back at Kenny, who was behind me and could see he too was holding his breath. Then suddenly, I became angry and exploded.

"Alice! You come out with your hands in the air!" Kenny joined in behind me, yelling, "Show yourself, Alice! Right now!"

We advanced down the stairs and I could see the coal furnace with a few lumps of coal scattered on the floor directly in front of it. There was a large coal bin behind a partial wood partition, also with lumps of coal on the floor in front of it. I froze again as I stepped to the floor at the bottom of the stairs. I could hear slow, measured breathing somewhere in front of me, and I knew where it was coming from.

Alice was hiding in the coal bin!

Though I couldn't see her, I knew she was there, hiding behind the partition. Kenny and I both began shouting at her: "Come out of there Alice with your hands in the air! NOW!" The fact that we called her by name so many times may have impacted her decision to finally show herself. Alice emerged from the coal bin looking like a bloody apparition in her bloodstained pale dress.

Her dark face was smeared with blood, coal dust, and shimmering with dripping sweat. She had thoughtlessly brought us to her own home, and had to know she was *not* going to get away with her crime spree, and yet she was *still* defiant. With the razor glittering in her right hand, I heard myself shouting at the top of my lungs: *"Drop the razor or I'll blow your fuckin' head off, Alice!"*

We stood twelve feet apart and I was angry and fed up. I was also exhausted *and* hungry. My .38 service revolver was cocked, my arms outstretched, holding the gun with the barrel of the gun pointed directly at her throat.

My thoughts were rushing about what she had done and all the violence and mayhem she had created in less than an hour of time. She was a danger, to the public and to herself. Alice had slashed her boyfriend, Napoleon, where I don't know, but he was in bad shape. That assault was a felony, then she'd slashed the security guard, another felony, and then hijacked a taxi, threatening the driver with the same straight razor, also another felony. I had *no* intention of being the next victim of Miss Alice Johnson.

I was never more ready to kill someone than I was at *that* moment in 1962.

Both our flashlights illuminated Johnson's face as she stared at me and the gun barrel. I watched her eyes slowly transform, it was a slow shift from glaring at me, to looking down at the floor. I watched her expression change from arrogant defiance to uncertainty. Her body began to relax and her shoulders slumped. She dropped her head and I heard the straight razor fall to the floor with a welcome clank. At that point, she looked up at me, her shoulders hunched. She was defeated and now suddenly, Alice was also very frightened.

Reality was sinking in. Finally!

Her crime spree was over and she would have to face the music. Her man "Napoleon," would likely be gone to her forever, and move on to the next woman. She would lose her home and all her possessions, such as they were. Alice's life would take a dramatically different turn once she was booked into the Police Headquarters building downtown and sent directly into a new and uncertain future in the Oregon prison system.

I told her to put her arms up above her head and *keep* them up. She nodded her head and whispered *"okay, officer."* I walked over and picked the razor up off the floor, flipped it closed, and slipped it in my right front pocket, all while keeping a sharp eye on Alice with her arms raised to the ceiling. Kenny and I each grabbed an arm, and hustled her up the stairs.

We told her if she behaved herself, we wouldn't have to cuff her until we got outside next to the car. That may sound strange given modern police protocol but it *was* what Kenny and I decided to do. Somehow, we understood she was not going to run.

We also knew she was eager to comply and that we had the situation under control. As we were taking her to our police car a photographer from the *Oregonian Newspaper* began to take photos of us while we walked down the street. A short article with our photo appeared in the *Oregonian* the following day explaining that Miss Alice Johnson would be spending several years in prison for slashing two men, a black man and a white man and threatening to slash another white man with her straight razor. If ever a woman was a danger to herself and others, it was Miss Alice Marie Johnson in 1962!

Kenny Zap and I had made the local paper, though I wouldn't learn of this for over fifty years because I was too busy working answering radio calls and trying to make Portland streets safe for citizens and was rarely one who had the time to read the daily newspaper.

* * * *

Over the intervening decades I've often thought how glad I was that Miss Alice Johnson decided *not* to die in that cold dark basement at 3540 North Mississippi Avenue that crazy summer night. In an article published with the *Oregonian* several weeks after her arrest, it was reported that Alice Marie Johnson, age twenty six, was sentenced to almost ten years in prison for her wild crime spree. To me that was a good thing because she had proven she was one dangerous woman, capable of extreme violence to those close to her and the general public at large.

While conducting research for this story and verifying that my memory of this event was accurate, my wife Theresa and I knocked on the door of 3540 North Mississippi Avenue in late December 2019. We were greeted by one Mr. Lafayette Keaton who was gracious enough to come out and sit on the front porch and speak with us at length about the history of the house and his own colorful, rather fascinating life.

Lafayette told us he was almost ninety years old and had lived in the house over fifty years. I told him how I had to arrest Miss Alice Johnson in the basement of his house in 1962. He told us he remembered Alice Johnson, and had purchased the house from a relative of hers for $6,000 probably sometime after she had been arrested. As Alice went to prison, she would have had no way to continue the mortgage payments, if she even owned the house. Alice went to prison for close to ten years for her violent assaults, Lafayette got the house, and I didn't have to kill anyone, so it all worked out in the end.

Villa St. Rose and Van's Olympic room

The building still sits impressively on a large lot at 597 North Dekum Street, the Villa St. Rose in the Piedmont neighborhood of Portland. Back when I was a street cop, all during the 1960s, the Piedmont district was a neighborhood of older homes, parks and Mom and Pop grocery stores that separated the dangerous Albina ghetto and the equally dangerous St. Johns neighborhoods from each other.

The Villa St. Rose had ivy-covered brick buildings which were centered on a central courtyard of well trimmed grass, flowers and religious icons, like statues of Mother Mary with baby Jesus. At the time I worked in that district, Villa St. Rose was a home for what we called "wayward girls," many of whom were simply abused and neglected kids, finally becoming runaways, pregnant, or both.

The courtyard, beyond the front door of the building, was an area to relax and meditate in, and I would occasionally see nuns praying there. There were picnics in the courtyard for the troubled girls who lived there, and for their families, all while they were kept under the close supervision of the nuns, who were well aware that most of the girls were abused and neglected. Villa St. Rose was an accredited high school and living facility staffed by nuns of the *Order of the Good Shepherd* and other professional social service workers. As many as two hundred girls resided at the facility at any one time.

My interaction with the facility occurred when my partner and I had to deliver a teenage girl in handcuffs, to the intake nun on night duty, as we both worked the graveyard shift. Our patrol district always included Albina, a neighborhood whose economy was fueled by heroin, prostitution and alcohol—alcohol which was available at any tavern or bar regardless of how old you were. If you could sit upright on the bar stool, and were not a small child, you would be served. I often saw teens, 15, 16 and 18 being served alcohol, usually beer. And naturally heroin was also available for the asking, though that was usually purchased by kids in their twenties. Alcohol *and* heroin could be yours if you had the money and it generally didn't matter if you were underage.

The young girls we took to Villa St. Rose were all victims of abusive parents, or a home with *no* responsible adult, sometimes just surviving with an aunt or uncle, while the parents were away, often in prison. The girls came from homes of extreme poverty with disorganized or nonexistent social structure. They were left to their own devices and or wits, which often lead to alcohol and marijuana use as well as the increasingly trendy LSD which became popular during the 1960s and the burgeoning Hippie scene. Most of the girls were Black and a smaller number of Native American girls too, but I escorted white girls to Villa St. Rose as well.

I would listen to the handcuffed girls in the back seat of my police car many times crying as they shared sad stories of no heat in the house, and nothing to eat but maybe some peanut butter and jam with a spoon. I would listen to how stepfathers and mothers would fight after getting drunk, spending their paycheck on booze and then begin cussing and slapping their children. "I can *never* do anything right and then I get beat up for it," I heard between the tears and sobs of one poor Black girl. "So I crawl out my bedroom window and I run away. I go to my boyfriend's house and smoke some weed. His cousin makes home brew and we get drunk on it, sometimes. It's better than bein' at home."

The girls I came across in my patrol district were victims of poverty, and social dysfunction as well as their own raging hormones. The teenage girls had virtually nothing, and so went looking for teenage boys, and the boys were *always* willing.

Policy dictated we never take the handcuffs off until the girls were safely inside the front door of Villa St. Rose. The nun would take out her pen, and enter the girl in a log book and then escort the young woman, sometimes pregnant, to a room where she could shower, get into clean underclothes and a nightgown, get a bowl of hot soup, bread and butter and then into a clean warm bed.

After signing the girl in, the nun and I would look at each other and perhaps chat for a moment. The nuns at the Villa St. Rose always seemed full of compassion and weariness at the plight of these poor girls. I often saw sadness in their eyes and a sense of hopelessness pass over their faces if I brought in the same Black girl more than once. Delivering wayward girls to Villa St. Rose in the middle of the night was hard on *my* psyche too, and I always hoped for another radio call right away, so I had something else to think about besides those lonely isolated girls with their sad dark eyes and no one in their corner. Sometimes I'd try to counsel the girls, encouraging them to stay in the home. "Stay here with the nuns, go to school, try to make it work *for* you. At least you'll have a bed to sleep in and food to eat." Often as not the girls wouldn't hear a word I'd say.

Too often the next call would be another family beef. Domestic disturbances or "Family Beef," calls as radio dispatch and every other cop I knew referred to them were all too frequent. In my patrol district of the Albina ghetto we averaged about one of these calls per shift, sometimes more. I worked graveyard so by the time my shift began a lot of alcohol had gone down the throats of the residents and a lot of heroin up their noses or injected into their veins. The fights were usually caused by too much drinking, though.

One longtime resident of North Mississippi Avenue, which was part of my district, and a personal friend, told me recently that living there in the sixties was like the *"Wild West out there at night."* When the sound of gunfire erupted: *"We headed for the basement. Because the bullets couldn't come through the concrete."* He was right. Albina and the St. Johns area was like the *Wild Wild West* of early America in those days of the sixties.

The family disturbances we were called to always seemed to be within the many derelict wood frame houses that dotted the Albina ghetto by the hundreds. They were owned by slumlords or residents who could never afford to maintain them and they were often repossessed by the banks. The kitchen floors all had fifty-year old linoleum worn through to the subflooring, and it seemed there was always a kitchen sink full of dirty dishes, with a continuously dripping faucet.

Old electric range stovetops with two burners missing and dirty skillets, or old pans resting against a wall with dried splashes of something cooked a long time ago, was a common sight. Broken and stained furniture sat on dirty hardwood flooring. There was often a large wooden cable reel for a coffee table or a couple of pieces of plywood set up on bricks or concrete blocks for a shelf to hold canned food. Broken windows held in place with duct tape and covered by stained draperies usually completed the living room decor.

In the winter the entire family would be huddled in one room heated by an electric space heater as heating oil and coal were usually too expensive to buy. Some of the better houses in that area might have a fireplace and they would be burning wood in them, sometimes the damp wood from backyard trees they would chop down in desperation, or discarded pallets they'd go out and collect on the streets.

It is no wonder that many of the girls I transported to Villa St. Rose wanted to crawl out their bedroom windows and run away. What little family income there was usually went first to the man of the house for his "get highs," usually booze or drugs, and money for the poker games at the after hours clubs. The women were mostly black women, but there were some white women living with black men, and a few Mexican women as well.

The women were the only stability in these families but that's not saying much because so many of the mothers were also alcoholics and drug addicts. Welfare money, and food stamps were usually the only money that brought food and clothing into the household, supplemented by food boxes from churches and what the police officers brought out each shift from the *Portland Police Sunshine Division.*

My partner and I regularly delivered large food boxes to these residences when we could see nothing in the refrigerator except perhaps a can of beer, a half a bottle of Tequila and a withering onion or year old potato shriveling in the salad crisper.

On one occasion in the early 1960s, perhaps 1964, I recall seeing two small Black children huddled in a corner, sitting on a blanket, no older than five and six. They were wearing worn, dirty clothes, which were no more than rags, and with no shoes or socks on their feet, I could see they were cold and hungry. They stood sharing the contents of a long packet of *Saltine Crackers,* an older brother caring for his little sister, each sharing the crackers fairly, one for him, one for her. They were frightened that the police were in their home and I could tell, they were embarrassed, too.

I took the mother aside in the hallway and quietly scolded her. I told her she could do better than that. That she needed to provide food for her children and at least socks for their feet during the cold of winter. But she was drunk and didn't seem to hear a word I said, her eyes dull, not perceiving what I was trying to convey to her. She shrugged and said they were okay and she had grown up under worse conditions. I ended up calling for the *Women's Protective Division* on the patrol car radio, and the children were taken to one of the Kerr Orphanages. There they would be bathed, clothed, fed and fitted with warm socks, and shoes until hopefully other arrangements could be made with other family members more able or interested in caring for them. This happened frequently, even back in the sixties a lot of decent Black grandmothers and aunties were raising their children's or sibling's children.

Witnessing the way children, Black, white, and Native American were mistreated, neglected and abused was hard on me and every other cop I knew. And seeing it so often, year after year, frankly, it wears you down. No one understands this better than another police officer who has seen it too, year after year.

When it came to domestic violence calls, if the couple were fighting when we arrived, we separated husbands from wives or girlfriends from boyfriends and served as referee until we could find out why the police were called, and what if anything could be done to resolve the problem. Most often both parents had been drinking which led to arguments, which then lead to blows, then an injury and then the neighbors calling the police due to the racket and of course the crying bewildered children.

I would always try and counsel these women, who were victims of circumstance, poverty, and a poor environment. I offered alternatives to them getting beaten up all the time. I provided phone numbers for social service agencies where they could get family counseling together or individually. I told them where they could get food boxes, food stamps, and free clothing at some local area churches. I sometimes told them to fight back against abusive husbands or boyfriends, with a baseball bat, not the wisest course of action as many of these women were routinely battered by the disturbed alcoholic men in their lives.

My efforts were usually to no avail as we returned many times to the same house and for the same reasons. Too often, for some women, accepting beatings on a daily or weekly basis was easier than jumping out on their own, getting a job, finding an apartment to rent and making their own decisions. And most of these women simply had nowhere else to go, no education and little to no family support.

It was a time when police could *not* make an arrest on an assault they did not witness or if the spouse refused to press charges. It was rare when a victimized spouse followed through and signed a complaint with the City Attorney at the DA's office. The poverty was so great and the alcohol and drugs so prevalent I felt each new working day would be a rerun of the last shift. I felt a great deal of personal frustration trying to counsel these adult women and young girls because what they needed was far more complex and involved than anything I could ever offer them. In many ways it felt like spitting against the wind.

* * * *

In 1961, I was a 25-year-old rookie, a raw, inexperienced recruit assigned with a veteran officer as my training coach on the graveyard shift. We were assigned to patrol the Albina ghetto, definitely the toughest part of town in the 60s. My uniform was new and shiny and I was looking at a year of probation before I would be on my own. My job was to observe, learn and have no opinion of my own. Usually our first stop of the evening was Van's Olympic Room, a tough, Black-only bar *unless* you were a white man and looking for a pretty Black or biracial hooker.

Van's was located on North Vancouver Avenue and Fremont Street. I learned as time went by that Van's was a front for heroin and prostitution. The bar was owned by Elwin Van Riper, a white man and managed by Leroy Clarke, a Black man. Leroy was smooth skinned; with straightened black hair slicked back with scented hair grease. Leroy was good looking with even white teeth and referred to as "pretty," by the many women who admired him.

He was also a heroin dealer and a pimp.

It was at Van's where I first saw Thelma Moody in 1961. She was dancing on top of a grand piano near the bar, nude except for a G-string and pasties covering her nipples. Thelma was beautiful with velvety brown skin, beautiful voluptuous breasts and thighs. She moved like she had no bones in her body. She wiggled like a beautiful snake. Patrons would tuck folding money in her G-string as she danced, while she beckoned them just close enough to tuck the money in. I was taken by her beauty and perfect body as most men were, both white and Black. Thelma was a stunner.

I had never been around Black people much, though I did have a Black best friend in high school for a couple of years during which we hung out regularly, even after graduation, but I still didn't know many other Black people. And there I was, in 1961, thrust into this new world of Black culture, which included alcohol, heroin, prostitution and crime.

Thelma was only 19-years-old, not quite old enough to be in a bar, but I didn't know it and my partner/coach never mentioned her age until much later on. Thelma was also a heroin addict, with a pimp named Jaynolen Moody, and he kept her supplied in heroin. They lived together in a house near NE 14th and Alberta Street and naturally were never married, though she did take his last name.

Another pimp heroin dealer of the time was Buck Owens, who my partners and I sometimes called "Dumbfuck Buck." He had two other Black women working for him: Pam Owens who had the narrow features of an Ethiopian princess, with a thin nose and beautiful sculpted lips, and Myra Owens, another Black woman. Both were strikingly beautiful. They were both teenagers when I first encountered them in the clubs along Williams Avenue and clearly not old enough to be drinking in a club.

Since I was a probationary officer, my three months of exciting duty in Albina was followed by a boring three months working in the city jail as a jailer, which I hated and an equally boring time working as a police records clerk. After that I was assigned to the Traffic Division working traffic accidents with an old timer coach.

Chasing traffic violators and investigating accidents *was* exciting and rewarding especially when we took a drunk driver off the streets. We felt like many idealistic cops, that we were making the world a safer and better place and it was a good feeling for a long time. Until such time that it was *not* a good feeling anymore, and I felt like nothing I was doing would make one whit of difference in the long run.

But my heart wanted to go back to Albina as a district officer. That's where the action was and where you could make "the good arrests" as one of my supervisors called them. After being a traffic cop I did a stint as a Vice officer spending way too much time in the downtown dive bars, like *The Viking* on Third and Burnside, which is now currently *Dante's Inferno*.

I spent my time in these dives looking for hookers and illegal gambling games as well as watching the drugs and alcohol economy humming along undisturbed by either police or community concern. Booze and heroin cut a wide swath of misery and human destruction, but no one seemed to care. Neither did the police brass and most especially *not* the city council or politicians.

For a long time I wondered why the police did nothing about the lawlessness in Albina as well as St. Johns which created so much chaos and suffering among regular working people. It took me a while to figure it all out.

But I did.

In 1964 I was able to get myself transferred to North Precinct which controlled the area of Albina where I wanted to work. That area was Williams Avenue where most of the criminal nightclubs operated and the street officers commonly referred to as *"The Avenue."*

The night Sergeant thought I might not be tough enough to take on the Albina ghetto and insisted I work car 43 in downtown St. Johns to prove myself. The first month I arrested thirty nine people on warrants just checking bars and talking to people. It seemed like *everyone* in St. Johns was wanted for something.

My activities caused a lot of "grousing" and complaining from the other ten officers, all of them old timers from the 1940s on the graveyard shift and preparing for retirement. I had arrested more people in one month than the other ten officers on the shift had done in *six* months of working.

I was upsetting the apple cart and I was beginning to see the overall problem. The officers were *not* doing their jobs. To say they were apathetic would have been a huge understatement.

After roll call and a quick stop for a cup of bourbon laced coffee at any number of lounges, the old timers would head to their favorite hiding spots and sleep through the night. Patrolling the neighborhoods and doing community policing was of no interest to them.

Police work at that time in the 1960s was often considered a part time job and the graveyard shift was the favorite shift of those "part time cops." There were a lot of parks with wooded areas and places under the St. Johns Bridge where they could sleep in the back of their squad cars, with a pillow under their heads and covered up by a cozy woolen blanket. Then after waking to the sun, they would head to breakfast and go to their regular daytime jobs. It was a great con job and many police officers were making double the money from not doing their job as police officers.

It always seemed horrible to me that these guys could do this and not hate themselves for it later. They had no interest in making the world a better place. All they wanted was another paycheck for doing nothing all night. These were the kinds of guys who would just ignore code 3 emergency calls.

After three months of working car 43 and proving I could do it, my sergeant agreed to give me the Albina patrol district I told him I wanted. I believe it was partly to get rid of me as the older officers wanted me gone from St. Johns, and refused to work with me, ignoring me, glaring at me and not speaking to me. I was keeping them awake at night answering calls and being on the radio all the time. *I was working* and *they* weren't.

By now I had acquired a good partner, Officer Ray Jones. Together we shook our heads at all the lazy cops we saw employed within PPB, and the broken system which allowed it to go on. Sleeping all night and not doing police work during the midnight hours was *not* making Portland citizens safe.

Over coffee at Devlin's Café on our first night working Albina, Ray and I sat down and talked. We vowed to begin enforcing the laws in Portland. We were both young and idealistic and we wanted to make the world a better place. We saw working together as a way to make a good sized dent in the suffering of the hardworking resident Black folks, which was allowed by the rampant lawlessness that made up the Albina neighborhood. There were many good Black families that were law abiding, worked at regular blue collar type work, attended church and tried to raise their children well.

At the very edge of our district at North Vancouver and Fremont Street was Van's Olympic Room. We began our efforts there. We entered our first shift together, and after a cup of coffee at the bar which we *paid* for, Ray and I began checking out the crowd and watching Thelma Moody dance on the top of the old battered Grand piano. By now she was twenty one and old enough to actually *be* in Van's legally. Thelma was still beautiful, but drinking, dancing, using heroin and being a prostitute was slowly stealing her looks and her vitality. She was noticeably thinner than when she was nineteen and not as friendly either.

As we walked in, and she saw us, she stopped dancing and stood watching us silently, glowering hatefully at us until Le-Roy motioned to her silently with his hand, to keep on dancing. We moved among the drinkers, shouldering our way through, checking the ID of anyone who looked underage and introducing ourselves to the patrons.

"Hello! How ya doin? I'm Officer DuPay and this is Officer Jones!"

We worked our way through the crowd, and noticed several people suddenly leaving via the back door. I nudged Ray and we smiled and chuckled. Two uniformed police officers checking ID's made the management nervous and quickly put a damper on the atmosphere of merriment and fun. Underage drinkers and those holding *smack* for sale had apparently decided it would be better to leave. I had a brief conversation with both Mr. Van Riper and Leroy "pretty boy" Clark as he was sometimes called. We informed them we would be coming in on a nightly basis from now on, and underage drinkers would be arrested and as a result Van's Olympic Room could lose its liquor license if they let the underage drinking continue.

Our advice was largely ignored—at first, but in time they learned to take us seriously. The next bar in need of corrective action was King's Tavern just a few blocks from Van's on North Williams Avenue. We did the same walk through, checking ID's and explaining to the manager that they could no longer serve alcohol to people who were already drunk. I recall vividly the first time Ray and I walked in, and how the manager was flabbergasted and defiant. *"We've always done it this way!"* he complained. *"They come here to get drunk!"* We could see the lawlessness tolerated for years was going to be a serious challenge to turn around.

The cards were stacked against us, too, in other ways. Our own Captain, "Diamond Jim" Purcell Junior, the disgraced former Chief of Police was operating two whorehouses in Albina. This was allowed by Mayor Terry Shrunk, who was happy to keep most vice and drugs contained in Albina and St. Johns if it meant the southeast side of town and the west hills and NW remained protected from the scourge of heroin. The underlying reality of this contradiction was based in racism, but in those years racism was not something most people even talked about.

For these and many other reasons the older officers felt they could sleep on the job at night with no need to enforce the law, *if* they worked at North Precinct. Mayor Shrunk and Captain Purcell didn't care that much if there was law and order in the North End because they benefited from the vice that occurred there every day financially and in other ways. Of course rapists, child molesters and murderers were arrested and incarcerated but other crimes of less consequence were largely ignored, which included prostitution and low level drug dealing.

But we did have some success. Van's was closed twice for selling to minors sometime after Ray and I began making our visits. King's Tavern was closed intermittently for serving drunks and once for failing a health department inspection. The Red Sands night club at NE Union and Shaver Street was permanently closed sometime around 1965 because of the regular drunken brawls and near riots that spilled out onto Shaver Street on weekends, stopping traffic and creating havoc with stabbings and shootings.

But we could never stop the heroin traffic and distribution. It was beyond our ability as street cops. The influx of Chinese imported heroin, (beginning in the early 1900s when Opium was popular) had been going on for so many decades, and was so entrenched in the Albina area and within the Black community, that stopping it was next to impossible during the 1960s. It was a case of supply and demand.

In the four years Officer Ray Jones and I spent working Albina we watched Thelma Moody, Pam Owens and Myra Moody deteriorate from beautiful young women to hollow eyed, depressed, and sallow faced shadows of their former selves. For me it was painful to watch.

The pimps who controlled their lives fed off of them in the same way a *vampire bat* drinks blood from a host. Pimps were the truest example of a low level parasite. They were blood suckers and Ray and I *despised* them. They had no honor, no work ethic and they had no regard or genuine affection for women. They were only too happy to ruin their lives for money.

The fast life effectively burned those once beautiful girls up. I watched as the heroin stole their souls, their decency and their self-respect. Thelma was shot and killed by Myra in Van's Olympic Room in 1974 over an argument over "the quality" but likely the ownership of a cheap ten dollar wig. Thelma went to the morgue and Myra went to jail for a few weeks before it was decided the shooting was self-defense and Myra was freed.

I heard through the cop grapevine that Pam Owens died of an overdose before she was 21, which I always thought a tragedy, but I've also heard that she may have lived, too. Either way,

Pam was exquisitely beautiful and should have been given help, despite her addictions. She had the face of a film star and if I could compare her to anyone it would be the Hollywood actress, Halle Berry, although truthfully, I believe *Pam* was prettier.

In 1977 the heroin dealer LeRoy Clark was shot and killed in Van's Olympic Room by the Portland Police SWAT team over what I believe was a drug deal gone bad. Narcotics Sergeant Charlie Hill, a dirty cop if there ever was one, was shot too, by LeRoy, but Hill survived. Later in an *Oregonian* newspaper article, Hill was quoted as saying: "I lost a friend today," referencing the death of LeRoy Clark, which was an immediate signal to me that Hill was involved in the illegal drug trade.

LeRoy was a pimp and a drug dealer, but he was also Hill's friend? Hill's thoughtless admission was a red flag. Criminal activity made Van's Olympic Room a sleazy and dangerous place and it remained so for years after I was gone. But more on LeRoy and Charlie Hill, later on in the final section of this book.

In 1967 I was promoted to detective and my responsibilities were no longer in Albina. Officer Ray Jones remained a street officer and continued to work in St. Johns but he never tried to advance through the ranks.

Sometimes, I wonder if Thelma, Myra and Pam had been white girls, would the reaction to the heroin trade in Albina have been different, considering their addiction? Would there have been a huge cry of outrage? Would there have been citizen indignation and a call to save these poor white girls? Ultimately neither the Black or white communities, nor the police really seemed to care that much, which always perplexed me.

That is why the law was largely unenforced in Albina and St. Johns at that time. Black pimps were more than happy to destroy the lives of their neighbor's daughters and get those girls hooked on smack and prostituting. The girls would end up lost in an endless cycle of dependency and despair, until they were no longer pretty enough to hook, at which time they were thrown away and sometimes even murdered.

Prostitution was *not* a victimless crime when I worked the streets of Albina. There were so many women and underage girls lost to the drug addiction and prostitution there, that I lost count of the ones I saw destroyed by it.

* * * *

"Mama won't come out!" was the nature of a call I received one night working alone in Albina in the late sixties. The call came from an old wood frame house which sat up on a bank back from the street on North Borthwick Avenue. At the door I was met by an angry and crying white woman in her forties. "Mama's locked herself in the bathroom and she won't come out. She's not even answering me!" she told me, anxious and upset. After coming into the house, I found the bathroom and knocked on the door asking the woman to come out. After several minutes of no response it was obvious something wasn't right.

"I think something's wrong with your mother. I'm going to have to force the door open. Is that okay?"

With her permission I easily pushed open the old wood frame door with my shoulder. As the door swung open we could see why Mama didn't answer. Mama was dead. It was a pitiful sight. The old woman was slumped over leaning to one side. Her pink panties were down around her ankles and her feet were still in blue fuzzy slippers. Her head had fallen back, against the wall, and her mouth was open, her eyes staring, unseeing, up at the ceiling. The caller, who was the dead woman's daughter, screeched in agony as she slowly realized her mother was dead. She leaned into me and threw her arms around me. I stood there letting her sob into my shoulder for a moment before I reached in to quietly close the door.

I led the poor woman out of the hallway and eased her into the living room and into her well-worn leatherette easy chair, placing a knitted afghan over her lap. I was thankful my shoulder was no longer the recipient of her tears but still sad that she was so upset. I brought her the telephone from a table nearby, placed the receiver in her hand and suggested she call a family member.

These kinds of calls were always hard for me and I took a deep breath as I walked out to the patrol car, a few minutes later. The coroner was called after I notified radio that I had a dead woman ready for them to transport. When the two men from the coroner's office arrived, I shielded the daughter by standing near her, gently turning her around and distracting her with conversation so she wouldn't have to see her mother's body being stuffed into a zip up body bag and hauled out the front door, stiff and rigid with rigor mortis.

No crime had been committed here but the devastating loss of a mother was equally impactful as if the poor woman *had* been murdered. With the coroner's men gone and the daughter in the company of a neighbor lady, I quietly closed the front door and returned to my patrol car. I sat for a few minutes making notes in my notebook for my report, leaned back into the seat and reflected on what had begun as a routine call. The initial call about someone being locked in a bathroom had turned into something else entirely. I recalled the jarring sound of the woman's cries and weeping, as she stood close to me outside the bathroom. There were no dangerous women involved in this call but there were victims just the same. Time for reflection was always cut short by another radio call. Someone else was in trouble in Portland and needed the police.

* * * *

Two images which have burned into my memory refuse to leave. They are two images of broken women I cannot forget. I can still see her running toward my patrol car, naked and screaming: "He tried to kill me! He tried to kill me!" The woman, middle aged and white was hysterical with tears streaming steadily down her face mixing with the snot from her nose. Her face was contorted into a grimace of horror. She was slender and terrified, and kept looking over her shoulder at the house, hunched over, her arms and hands trying desperately to cover her nakedness, passing over her breasts and pelvis, but terrified that someone might run out and go after her again.

I felt so sorry for her.

I jumped out of the squad car, ran around to the trunk, and retrieved the blanket I knew was there. She approached me hunched over, pathetic and naked, and I wrapped it around the woman's shoulders and front, and helped her into the back seat. I leaned into the car to hear her. "She's been shot. My daughter! Oh my God, he murdered her!" she continued to wail "He killed her!" over and over again. The words came out in strangled gasps between jagged breaths, as she pointed at the house she had escaped from and gestured in an upward motion with her hands. "The bathroom!" she managed to choke out. "The upstairs bathroom!"

Leaving the woman in the safety of my patrol car I raced to the house, taking the stairs two at a time, and walked through the front door, which was hanging wide open. It was a large American FourSquare house, commonly built between 1890 and 1930. The house had three stories and several bedrooms. It fronted the sidewalk above a large lot and up several concrete stairs. As I walked in I saw the lights were still on and the feeling was eerie. There was no one else about, as the shooter had fled and there were no other relatives. The silence was deafening, without so much as a cat or dog wandering around, or even the radio or TV on.

Seeing the first floor was clear I ran up the stairs to the landing and ventured toward the bathroom. I slowly pushed the door open with my gun barrel and realized it was too late to save the poor daughter. The young woman's body was slumped over. She was wedged between the toilet and the bathtub. The woman had been wearing a tattered pink nightgown, something that should have been tossed out long ago, which was now dotted in blood from close range, high velocity blood splatter. She had been shot in the head at point blank range. A .30-30 rifle casing lay on the black and white tile floor, a few feet away.

The bullet had penetrated the right side of her head near the temple and completely blew away the back of her skull. The damage made her face and facial bones look as if they had just collapsed. She didn't look human anymore; instead she looked like a "bloody fright mask of someone with a deformed and concave face." The bullet had passed through the daughter's skull with such velocity, that there were bone fragments and pale gray brain tissue sticking to the green tile wall and the dingy mirror. (DuPay, 2015).

After I saw that the girl was dead, I jogged down the stairs and back out to the car to talk to the mother, still sitting in the backseat. The distraught mother told me her son-in-law had shot her daughter in a fit of jealousy in the upstairs bathroom. The dead girl's mother was weeping uncontrollably as I tried to get information from her.

I was 28-years-old and trying to console a woman in her forties who had just witnessed the murder of her daughter with a hunting rifle at close range. It was early fall and late at night so it wasn't hot, which I was grateful for, but I remember my heart was racing and I felt completely inept. There was nothing I could say or do to change anything. I couldn't comfort this poor woman who had just seen the most horrible thing a mother could witness—the murder of her own daughter.

Between her choked sobs she managed to tell me her daughter had wanted to escape an abusive marriage but the man decided to murder her instead. As I listened to her talk and ramble on brokenly, I picked up the mic and called it in, speaking quietly: "I have a homicide out here in St. Johns. I need the detectives right away."

One thing about this call that I never forgot or forgave is the fact that not *one* other North Precinct police officer employed with PPB, who was on patrol that night, covered me. *Not one.* They knew a woman had been murdered with a shotgun, and they knew that "DuPay" had taken the call, but they chose not to provide cover, which is unheard of in police work. Was I really that bad because I wanted to do real police work and make the world a better place? Interfering with their con job was enough for them to abandon all integrity and not respond to a code 3 call that night where another officer could have been in grave danger.

The shooter could still have been around, wanting to lop off a few more heads. That was a real possibility, but these "sleeping beauties," as I called them, were willing to let a dedicated police officer, one of their own "brothers" face such risk alone. Simply because I took my work seriously, and *they* ended up looking bad as a result? Their cowardice and unprofessionalism was unquestioned that night as I stood there, alone, silently fuming. I was the new guy who was working, and making them look bad when they would rather grab their pillow and blanket from the trunk, and perhaps down a shot of whiskey to help them sleep.

I stood on the sidewalk, alone that night, looking around, wondering if the man with the rifle was lurking nearby in the shadows of an old Maple tree, and waited for the detectives to arrive. I knew the man was long gone and would likely be found later, so I wasn't worried he was still nearby, but he *could* have been nearby and a clear and present danger.

It took almost fifteen long minutes for the detectives to get to

St. Johns from the downtown precinct and I remember how quiet it was as I stood there alone outside the patrol car, listening to the muffled sound of the mother crying and crying inside the car.

There was no one about and the stillness was unnerving. This was a large area with dozens of houses, and not *one* single neighbor came outside to inquire what the commotion was about, or to offer the woman any kind of aid or solace after her daughter had been murdered by a gunshot blast. Ultimately, being ignored by my fellow North Precinct officers was their way of putting me in my place. They didn't like me because *I* worked all night and *they* didn't, but I didn't care what they thought of me. I was going to change the world. I was going to make the world a better place, or so I thought.

I remember I was glad to be rid of this call, and turn it over to the dicks in Homicide. It was a horrible thing for a young man of only 28 to see. To think that a man could murder his wife with a .30.30 rifle at close range and annihilate her face and head was something I could not wrap my brain around.

The image of the bone chips and bloody brain matter running down the mirror and tile wall remain forever etched in my mind. I try not to think of the poor girls body stuffed between the toilet and tub, her life snuffed out. But I can't make the memories go away either, nor will I ever be able to forget the broken mother, who was driven nearly mad by what she had just seen.

Because I had such a close and healthy relationship with my own mother, Clara DuPay, I have always felt a strong sympathy, affection and feeling of protectiveness toward women. Dealing with women, as a police officer, could be a challenge for me, as it can be for any police officer. In general it was always easier dealing with women than having to contend with combative, rambunctious and defiant men, some of whom personified absolute evil in the flesh.

CHAPTER 3

TWO PLUS ONE EQUALS MURDER: LOSING ARTENT THOMAS

"There is no trap so deadly as the trap you set
for yourself."
—Raymond Chandler, *The Long Goodbye*

It was the middle of May, 1980, and I was in a dismal looking Seattle morgue.

"She was stabbed 27 times," the Seattle detective told me over the phone. "And beaten up. The body's in pretty bad shape. She fits the general description of the woman you reported missing to the Portland police though, late 20's, Black, short hair. She was probably about 5 feet 6. Most of her clothes were torn off when

Artent Thomas in a glamor shot.

she was found dumped in the bushes in that Park. We'd appreciate it if you could come up to Seattle and identify the body. Tire tracks were found nearby. She may have been dumped out of a car."

That would explain the extra 200 or so miles on my car, a trip from Portland to Seattle, and back. She told me she was going to visit a girlfriend but I knew it was probably cocaine she was after. "I'll be there first thing in the morning. My mom will drive me up," I said. I felt heartsick and was too upset to drive to Seattle by myself, or to even *drive* for that matter. I prayed the body they found of a young Black woman was *not* my precious Artent.

I've never known a woman before or since with the name "Artent," but somehow it fit her. She was different. She 'zinged' my heart when I first saw her. Pretty legs, warm brown skin, with lots of red lipstick. In high heels she looked like "Minnie Mouse" and I used to tease her about it. People at the clubs said she had perfect "disco hips" and a hell of a butt. Her breasts were large for the rest of her frame, which included a small waist, and she always showed a lot of cleavage. So much so, that sometimes one of her nipples would slip out of her bra. When that happened, she flashed an irresistibly sultry smile and tucked it back in making sure an audience was watching.

It was 1977 and I was working as a detective, when I first met Artent through a mutual friend. There was an *instant* attraction between us, kind of a love-at-first-sight thing. She felt it as much as I did. She was a different kind of Black Portland girl, though. The fact that I was a police detective didn't matter to her. She was attracted to me and she knew my wife had just left me for a woman, so I think she felt sorry for me, too.

Artent was beautiful, sexy to the nines and a *whore*—an old school police term for a drug addicted prostitute. She wiggled her sexy way into my life when it was in turmoil. I had found my wife of twenty years in bed with a lesbian woman, Claudia, who often had some good cocaine. I thought Claudia was our friend, but she had her sights on my wife and would end up paying for the divorce so they could be together. It helped to explain the reason my wife had become more and more distant over the years. I thought maybe it was just boredom. But a lesbian? No wonder I couldn't turn her on anymore. It wasn't *me* she wanted, it was a woman.

The shock of losing my wife to a woman wore off after a while and in a way, I felt relieved. My first wife had been unfaithful to me so many times with men, including other police officers I knew, that I lost track of the actual number. We had had a dysfunctional marriage since the very beginning and I wanted out, too. I'd tried for years to make our marriage work, but the reality was I was spitting against the wind. I sure as hell had a lot of life still ahead of me and maybe now, just maybe, I could find a Black woman. I wanted a sexy Black woman in my life and Artent more than fit the bill. A police buddy of mine had introduced us when Artent was about 26 and I was 41.

I was a white man but after the divorce I let my feelings run. Back in the day when I'd been a street cop working vice, I spent a lot of time working the Black neighborhoods and bars. I had fallen in love with a beautiful, light-skinned Black table dancer named Pam, but had never acted on my impulses and of course Pam despised me because I was white *and* a cop. At the time, I was married and wanted to be faithful to my wife. But now, I decided if the opportunity ever came to be with a Black woman, I would jump at it.

A few days after I met Artent, I picked her up one night in my black Cadillac, from her NE Portland apartment on Glisan Street. We drove to a decent five story motel on Barbur Blvd in Tigard, so we could share some coke and get to know each other. After parking I checked in and got the key, a room on the first floor, next to the parking lot. This would be my chance I hoped and I knew the coke would make my dick hard. Artent tossed her leather purse on the king sized bed, and smiled at me. She then walked into the bathroom but left the door open for me to see. She stood in front of the sink and tied off her arm with a piece of rubber tubing she'd brought with her. I was fascinated watching her get ready to shoot up. In the bathroom mirror she grinned at my reflection. "Wanna try it with me?" she asked playfully. "It's *your* dope."

Jesus! My mind froze. I'd been a cop half my life and I knew better on all levels. I'd always been faithful to my wife, even when I worked Vice, but I was secretly attracted to cheap looking, crotch-tight women showing some sexy pantyline and jiggling boobs. As a street cop I'd loved talking to the hookers in my district with their sexy come hither walks and too much lipstick. I'd ask how they were doing, and they'd tell me their troubles, trying to flirt, but I'd never gone past small talk. Having sex with a prostitute seemed too out there for me, and I chose to never go there. Most prostitutes I saw weren't clean, and that was a concern. Things were different now. Artent was different, she was young and looked healthy, fresh and new.

"Wanna try it?" she repeated, motioning me into the bathroom with her head, her breathy little girl voice unthawing my brain freeze. God yes, I thought to myself! I walked into the bathroom and stood next to her. "Hook me up, baby. Treat your daddy right," I murmured, feeling mildly ridiculous using such out of character words. My heart started pounding in my ears, so loud I didn't hear what she said as she eased the needle into the big vein inside my left arm.

I could *taste* the coke!

The rush hit hard. How did the taste of the coke in the needle get from my arm to my taste buds so instantly? I didn't know what to expect, having never shot up coke before, but the feeling was erotic, intensely sexual and nothing like I had ever felt before just snorting the stuff. She tossed the needle in the sink and led me to the bed. I don't remember taking off our clothes, but we did. I saw the clean white sheets, her beautiful dark body, and my pale body on top of hers. It was slow motion and fast moving all at the same time. And then we were yelling hoarsely at each other, but it wasn't yelling. What are the involuntary sounds that happen when your nerves explode in orgasm? "God! God! God!" she seemed to scream, or was it me? I was in her and she was in me.

We floated somewhere in the ether for a while, our bodies entangled in each other, until we started to come down from the high. "Let's do it again baby, there's still a little powder left," Artent said. Without waiting for my answer she wiggled out from under me and dashed naked to the bathroom, returning with a paper cup full of water, the needle, and the rest of the gram in the wrinkled snow-seal container. Jesus! I couldn't take my eyes off of her bouncing boobs as she jiggled to the bathroom and back.

This time we sat on the edge of the bed while she tied me off. "Hurry!" I said, wanting to get the same feeling again and get my still hard dick back inside her. She inserted the needle and drew in a small amount of blood to make sure she'd hit the right spot. Satisfied, she hit the plunger. I got the taste and was off flying again to that unexplainable place you go when you're shooting coke. She did the same and was back under me in a flash, the needle and rubber tubing sliding silently to the floor. We made love for the rest of the night, dissolving into each other, color no longer mattering. Each thrust of my hips was met with her own push-back until our whispers crescendoed in simultaneous multiple orgasms.

Later, as we both relaxed in satisfied exhaustion, she offered me a Valium to help me come down from the coke. I took it and we smoked a bud of Maui Wowie from my weed connection in Hono. Sleep came after the second smoked joint. I pulled up the covers and cuddled close to this beautiful vision. One of my dreams had come true.

During this time in my life, in April of 1978, I chose to resign from the Portland Police Bureau because of my doctor's suggestions that I find other less stressful work. "One day you're gonna have to choose between the police department and your health, Don!" he told me, more than once as it turned out. The health issues included a bleeding ulcer, which required surgery, extremely high blood pressure and episodes of serious depression and melancholia. The world was full of misery and suffering, and nothing I did as a policeman or detective seemed to matter or make any kind of difference. I tried for a long time to make it work with PPB, but after a while, I realized my doctor was right. I needed to get out.

Once I was free and my ex-wife, her lesbian lover, and PPB were behind me, I pursued Artent full-time. After a couple of months of going to hotels I came to a decision one night. We were lying next to each other and it was after 2:00 am. I thought that I could either go home to my nearly empty apartment on

27ᵗʰ and Killingsworth, the place I had gotten after my wife and I split, or I could go to *her* place. Her apartment was located at 2512 NE Glisan Street and had a solitary palm tree which rested on the south side of the building. It was incredibly tall, sparse, and inexplicable looking. Most Portlanders knew about the "sick looking palm tree" on Glisan Street, as it was the only palm tree in the entire city at the time and had become something of a strange, albeit well-known landmark.

Artent had been wanting me to move in with her anyway, so that night we drove back to her place and settled in. She had hardly any furniture and slept on a mattress on the floor. I changed that. I brought over some of my own furniture and purchased some other small items like end tables, and lamps, that I knew she'd like.

After I moved into Artent's place, she made no bones about the fact that we were together and I was her "old man." She told me one night while we snuggled in bed that I was "the only white Daddy," who had ever made her come. The other white men she had been with were "selfish" but not me, she said. Still she was a hooker and our life was the night life…the fast life. We spent many nights at the nightclub called "The Great Gatsby," on NE Halsey at 102ⁿᵈ avenue. The music was loud, the disco balls spun beautifully, the colored lights flashed and all was wonderful with the world. At least that's how it seemed.

Artent kept wanting me to dance with her on the floor, but I was not a natural dancer, remember I'm white, and awkward doesn't describe how I felt when I tried to dance. Truth is I looked and felt stupid. That is until she got me loaded on booze and coke. We always parked my black Cadillac across the street in a vacant lot and between music sets we would use the back exit and run across the street. She was in her late 20s then and I was in my early 40s and still in good shape, but we *had* to run it seemed.

Sitting in the front seat we used a small flashlight to illuminate the water bottle we carried, the cooking spoon, the needles and the rubber tie-off tube. I never learned how to inject myself. Artent always fixed me. She almost never missed, even in the dim light of the car. When we finished shooting up neither one of us could remain still and we'd sprint across the street back to the club racing each other to the door. I still wonder why shooting coke made us both want to take off running, but it seemed to be a necessary part of the rush.

Most bar patrons were only allowed one "in and out" pass but Artent did coke with the owner of the Gatsby so we had a free pass to go in and out all night. And we did, shooting coke each time. But I'll tell you, when we returned inside the club I could dance my ass off and Artent seemed to approve. Nobody laughed. Either because I was as good as I thought I was, (Artent had shown me some moves) or it was because I was her "old man" and they didn't laugh out of respect for her.

As the night ended and the bartenders yelled out "last call!" My Artent always left with one or two guys, off to get more coke and money. Even though she was my "old lady" she was still a prostitute and always did her own thing. She would kiss me goodnight and stick a few bills in my shirt pocket, money she had hustled while at the Gatsby. "Later baby," she'd whisper. "I'll be home before daylight."

But she never was.

I'd stagger out the back door of the Gatsby to my Cad and drive home alone, to the apartment. I was usually so drunk and high I was seeing double. To solve that problem I would shut one eye. It seemed to work. Hard to drive when all you could see was two roads, multiple traffic signals and cars with four headlights.

My guts were torn up though, her leaving with other guys knowing she'd fuck them for money, coke and weed. She swore she always used protection in an effort to protect against venereal disease, but I had to wonder and the fact is, I knew I'd never know one way or the other.

Back at home, during one memorable night, I found a Valium in an ashtray and put it under my tongue to dissolve. She was what she was, a whore and I knew it the first time I slept with her. Still, I felt castrated. That night, when I had pulled into the driveway of the apartment I parked the long black Cad more or less between the two yellow lines of her parking space. Once inside the apartment I retrieved the gallon bottle of Chablis from under the kitchen sink and drank until I passed out on the living room couch.

****

I sat in the back seat of my mother's car during the trip to Seattle, hunched into my coat. She had brought *Vale,* her longtime boyfriend. After my father passed away in 1975, she'd met Vale, a retired Greyhound bus driver at a community center which offered Square dancing socials. I was glad she had found someone, as Vale turned out to be easygoing and personable. They both understood I was too distraught to drive so I sat in the back watching the signposts fly by. Still, I was impatient and nervous.

"Hurry up, Mom! Can't you go any faster?" I saw my mother's face in the rearview mirror, looking back at me. Her brow was furrowed as she shared my anguish, but was more worried about *me* than a woman she'd never met. I knew Mom was very disappointed in my lifestyle at that point and in my association with Black people. She couldn't figure out what had happened to her son, the cop, the detective she used to brag about to all her friends while they played cards and drank coffee. I wasn't sure what happened to him either. Part of it was a strong unfulfilled desire to be "Black" for a while, for what reason, I don't know.

Another part of my decline was the total disillusionment I felt with the *Portland Police Bureau*, and the corruption that couldn't seem to be avoided, the corruption no one seemed to give a shit about. After 17 years with PPB, I ended up a sad cliche, completely burnt out, cynical, emotionally dead to the job. I often asked myself what good I had *ever* accomplished. A part of me had just stopped caring. Part of it was also the allure of the fast life, the desire to just be 'the other side of the coin' for a while. The desire to do wrong, to get lost and be reckless. I'd been good for so many years, and now I wanted to be bad.

I knew my life was on a downhill slide, but I wasn't ready to stop skidding, yet. "Can't you find a decent *white* woman?" Mom had been asking me. Probably not, I wanted to answer, because I wasn't *looking* for a white woman. Yeah, I had received a proper 'white' upbringing, which meant I was told that Blacks didn't associate with white folks unless they were employees or working for them. That's what I'd been taught, but I always resented it. Shouldn't I be allowed to be friends with whomever I wanted? Even when I was in high school and had a Black male friend named Frank, my mother disapproved. My father understood and smiled when he saw Frank and I hanging out together but my mother would get upset and angry.

Still, on that drive to Seattle, Mom could see how distraught I was, fidgeting and rocking in the back seat. I knew she could only wonder at the reason Artent hadn't picked me up after my hernia surgery at Emanuel Hospital. I'm sure she suspected it had something to do with drugs.

A hernia operation on my right side had recently become necessary and arrangements had been made for me to have it done at Emanuel Hospital. The plan was for Artent to pick me up when I was released, after three days at the hospital. When the day came, I sat in the hospital waiting room in the obligatory wheelchair. The nurse had parked me where I could see Artent coming, if she drove near the waiting room entrance/exit.

Artent never showed up.

I waited several hours trying to fend off the nurses' questions. *Did I have a ride? Was I sure someone was coming?* Hell yes! My ride home had been planned weeks before I was admitted to the hospital. But where was she? Where was Artent? I was becoming irritated. Did she get high and forget about me? Did she pass out somewhere? Where was my silly Minnie Mouse, my pretty girl I couldn't live without?

Two more hours went by and I couldn't sit still any longer. The nurses looked at me like they wanted the wheelchair back and *me* gone. I felt abandoned and angry. Finally, I called a Broadway Cab, the only cab number I could remember and was delivered to the Paramount Apartments, which I had recently gotten us into. As the cab drove up to the apartment, I saw my car was in the parking lot. I paid the cab driver, and slowly walked to my car. As I leaned in, looking in the window, I saw that the keys were in the ignition. How strange, I thought. I checked the interior for any sign of Artent, her purse, the bottle of perfume she kept in a straw basket in the backseat with a lipstick and some earrings, her apartment keys, anything. But there was nothing. The items in the straw basket were suddenly missing. Why?

It was then that I noticed there was over 200 miles on the odometer that hadn't been there when I entered the hospital. I tended to keep track of the mileage when Artent had the car just to see what she was up to. Switching on the ignition I saw the Cad was almost out of gas. Apprehensive now, I walked around back and opened the trunk, not knowing what to expect, hoping it was empty. It was, but so was the apartment. It had been four days since I'd heard from her, so on June 18th I reported Artent as a missing person.

The next day the Seattle police called.

****

The room where I found myself, in the King County morgue, was cold as the detective in charge wheeled out the refrigerated body covered by a sheet. The cadaver gurney stopped in front of me and on it was a tag that read, "Jane Doe." As the detective yanked the sheet from the body, my face twisted up and tears instantly came to my eyes. I turned away and threw my arms around my mother, and clung to her like a child. I felt like I had been kicked in the guts. It was her! God damn it! It was Artent! I forced myself to turn back and look at her again, my face covered in tears.

Artent was barely recognizable. She'd been bludgeoned, beaten almost beyond recognition, and her once beautiful heart-shaped face, a face that I loved so much, was destroyed forever. I would learn it was May 14th, 1980 that my Artent had been tormented, tortured, and murdered. Whoever did this was a sadist. Her real hair was always cut neatly short, as she preferred wearing high quality wigs. But looking down at her, I could see her favorite wig was gone and her natural hair was covered in mud, and caked in blood. Her clothes were covered in mud and mostly torn from her body, which told me she had likely been raped.

Only one eye was visible from the destruction to her face. Her mouth was distorted in the agony of her violent death. Her lips were cut in places, and flattened in a grimace, her cold face and body having gone through rigor mortis. Her arms were bloody, from defensive wounds as she'd tried to protect herself from the knife. It looked like she had been cut all over and it was clear she had died face down in the mud. Dried blood was everywhere. It was horrible.

"I guess that's her?" asked the detective somberly as he observed my reaction.

"Yes...that's her!" I choked out. "Her name is...was...Artent Thomas... "

"I'm sorry, they haven't been able to...get to her yet. That's the way she came in."

"Yeah, I understand," I said, the words coming out in a hoarse whisper.

As a former police detective I had seen too many dead bodies already, but this bloody mess, this stiff and tortured corpse had been Artent.. My precious girl was gone. She had been a butterfly and now my beautiful butterfly was dead. I always feared her life on earth would be short. Somehow, I just knew. Her butterfly-self flitted here and flitted there, never stopping long in one place. Sometimes she landed on me and stayed a while and we had fun, but if I tried to catch her, she flitted away, smiling back at me over her wings.

Now, it was death that finally caught Artent. Her once beautiful body lay on the stainless steel table as if pinned there, a fragile specimen crushed in its capture.

"Are you her next of kin?" asked the detective.

"No, we weren't married, we were engaged… to be married. That would be her sister. I'll get you her name and address."

"Okay."

"Now, you tell *me* who killed her so I can blow the motherfucker away!" I said quietly. The Seattle detective was unmoved by my passionate threat. He'd heard many like it before.

"We're not sure yet, but now that you've identified her we *will* be working with the Portland police." He turned over the tag that read Jane Doe and wrote ARTENT THOMAS in capital letters with a black pen. The murdered girl in the Seattle park now had a name. He turned back to me, "I know this is hard," he said, compassion now in his voice, "but don't do anything stupid. We'll get him." I nodded and said nothing.

Get him before I do, I thought to myself.

The Portland cops fingerprinted my car the next day and found faint bloody prints belonging to a Black man Artent had known. The guy had only recently been released from the Oregon State Prison where detectives told me he had met Artent in the "co-ed pre-release unit."

So, that was the "friend" she was going to visit in Seattle. Artent never did tell me the name of the friend she was going to meet, just that it was an old "girlfriend" and she knew the woman was a good cocaine source. A half-truth to placate me and the truth is, I hadn't pressed her for details. I was in too much pain with my hernia and not thinking of much else.

A few months after we started living together in her Glisan apartment, Artent had gotten high and gone shoplifting at Nordstrom's department store at the Lloyd Center Mall. A store security guard spotted her stealing cosmetics, and clothes, and Artent, thinking her high-self could outrun the store cop, took off, sprinting out the door. "I can run *really* fast when I'm high!" I remembered her telling me once. I knew she was fast because when we'd shoot up coke when we went clubbing, we'd try and outrun each other to some imaginary finish line, laughing the whole time. Artent was fast but so was I, and I'd usually end up winning our races, just a few feet ahead of her.

But on that day, she'd stumbled in her high heels and the store cop caught her. This was back in the days when store cops could still physically restrain a shoplifter. He was probably sorry he got so close because Minnie Mouse beat him bloody using one of her high heel shoes as a weapon, pounding him on the head with it. She eventually got home, walking most of the way barefoot.

When Artent came down from her high at the apartment, she realized she'd dropped her purse with her Oregon ID inside. We both knew it was only a matter of time before she'd have to face charges. Eventually, her court appointed attorney (who was an old friend) told her over the phone that with her previous record for shoplifting and prostitution she would do some hefty time for "Theft and Assault" and she would need to turn herself in and face the charges. But we continued to party and stay high ignoring the real world for a while longer. When you're high it's easy to put off reality, at least for a while.

On a few rare occasions Artent would decide we needed to "take the day off," and we'd just have fun together. We would smoke pot and when the munchies overcame us, we loved to have breakfast at a little nearby cafe. She ordered her hashbrowns crisp and her eggs sunny-side up with white toast. "Please," and "Thank You," she always said, smiling pleasantly if it was a waitress, and sexily if it was a waiter. Artent was born to flirt and she loved *all* people, so I got used to it.

My meal was usually Pigs in a Blanket with lots of hot coffee to wash it down with. I would give her my little container of blackberry jam because she loved jam, and she'd put all of hers on her toast, spreading it thick and painstakingly to the very edge of the bread. I would watch her, smiling. No one could spread jam on toast like my sexy Artent could. Maybe it was just me, but I thought *everything* Artent did was sexy. After she spread the jam onto her toast, to her satisfaction, she would take a bite putting the jellied up corner daintily in her mouth. This woman gave me a hardon just watching her eat.

On one of those rare days off, after eating breakfast, I'd drive her over to Vancouver, Washington. About 6 miles up the freeway towards Seattle there was a little known turnoff that led to a private Arboretum. Some family had painstakingly, over the years, turned several acres of meadow and forest into a kind of wonderland of odd shaped trees, bushes and vines. It was pretty magical, especially if you were high. Some of the trees looked like ghostly shapes, some had animal shapes and there were some that looked like Christmas trees, but the "ornaments" were a different bush that had been grafted onto the 'Christmas' tree to look like it actually had ornaments.

My favorite little spot on the property, and the one we usually headed to, was about half a mile back on the trail, where a heart shaped tree was growing out of a lot of tall grass. We would make love on the ground hidden by the grass, our own private little piece of someone else's heavenly halfacre. But this time, in the hot summer, some asshole had mowed all the grass around the tree. We stopped abruptly, and looked at each other when we saw the tall grass was gone along with most of our privacy and wondered for a moment what to do next. But we shrugged it off. "We're so far back in here," Artent murmured, "no one will see us, anyway." I was hopeful. "Yeah," I answered, "no one will see us."

We grinned at each other, the prospect of making love out in the open, seemed to whet our appetite for each other and we took off running the rest of the way to the tree and fell to the ground laughing, rolling around and hugging each other. I took off my black leather jacket, the long one I had gotten when I was a detective with PPB, and put it on the ground for her to lay on. I lit a joint and we smoked it before taking one last look around, making sure we and the tree were alone.

Satisfied, Artent lay on her back, opened her arms to me and let me kiss her until most of her red lipstick was on me. Slowly, deliciously, my hand felt under her dress. I caressed her soft little vulva as she wiggled out of her panties. "Wait baby, we got a little powder to shoot up first," she whispered. Looking around, our privacy okay, I silently cussed the guy that cut our grass.

As luck would have it, I have a large vein running down the front of my penis. We had talked about it before, but this time we decided to inject the dope right into my dick. Artent called the big vein a "roller," because when she tried to hit it with the needle the vein moved. We persevered and after wiping off the tiny spot of blood from the injection site, I pushed it in her pussy as far as it would go.

We zoomed past heaven, flying right on by, kissing, rolling around on the ground, groaning and squirming, entwined in each other's body and lost to the world...until we heard voices coming down the trail toward us. The sound brought us both slamming back to earth. Two older white ladies were on a leisurely stroll up the path about 200 feet from us. We didn't think they had seen us yet, but my dick went limp instantly and her panties were back on in a flash. "Asshole grass mower," I said under my breath to Artent. "Let's get outa here!" We stood up and Artent lit a cigarette, coughing a little to let the intruders know someone else was in the area, as she wiped her face with a white tissue from her purse.

My dick hurt a little from the injection and a lot from not being able to come, as I also wiped my face with a cotton handkerchief I kept in my jacket, trying to get the red lipstick off. Artent was frustrated. "Let's go home and *do* it, baby!" she whispered to me, keeping her eyes on the trail. We smiled and waved politely at the two ladies as they passed. Artent had stopped for a moment and opened her compact mirror to finish wiping her face and refresh her lipstick, since most of it had come off on me. In her mirror she could see the ladies reflection and that they had turned around to look at us again, as they passed by. I knew they wondered what was going on, a gorgeous Black woman and a white man clear back here on the trail? Little did they know what a show they had just missed. Little did they know...

****

Have you noticed that courtrooms have their own smell, kind of woodsy and stale? Marble wall panels stare at you and you wonder how they got the slabs of marble carved so impressively. The hardwood benches seem to have absorbed years of the negative vibrations and nervous depressed energy of witnesses and victims, alike. The whole austere ritual of the black robed judge entering the courtroom to the words of the clerk, "All rise!" seems to be a tableau designed to impress and frighten all those who are seated, watching. A ritual of law that says none are above the black robed jurist staring down. Judges don't look down, they usually stare over their reading glasses, a habit enforced by old movies and Perry Mason TV episodes.

As a former street cop and detective with the Portland Police Bureau, I'd spent hundreds of hours in courtrooms. When I was a traffic cop, often violators would say: "I'll see you in court!" I'd laugh to myself, thinking: Sorry buddy, if you're not a plumber, don't try and fix your pipes, and if you're not an electrician, don't try and wire your house, and if you're not a judge, don't try and scare me by claiming your prowess in court. I make my living in court, asshole…that's where I make my fucking living.

Still, those were the old days, and Artent and I were in this courtroom to hear her sentence for stealing from the Nordstrom's and beating up their useless rent-a-cop. I was in a very familiar environment but in a very uncomfortable circumstance, this time. "Artent Thomas, I sentence you to three years in the Oregon State Prison for Theft and Assault." Her attorney nodded his head, acknowledging the judge's sentence as Artent jumped up, ridiculously proclaiming her innocence. "It wasn't me, Judge, I swear!" The judge furrowed his brow and took off his glasses, setting them down in front of him. He was fed up and I couldn't blame him. "I am as certain that you are as guilty of this crime, as I am certain that you are the *only* ARTENT Thomas in the entire state of Oregon! Judgment is entered. Deputies, take her into custody!"

The gavel slammed down on the hardwood desk and my pretty Artent was gone, looking back at me with big frightened eyes as the bailiff handcuffed her in front of me and whisked her away behind the big metal doors that I knew from years of experience led directly to the jail.

Reality was a motherfucker and the judge's gavel caught me

sliding into first base but both Artent and I had struck out. She would spend too many nights in a prison cell, for stealing overpriced cosmetics and clothes from the Nordstrom store, and I would be sleeping alone in our apartment in a pulldown Murphy bed with too many springs sticking up through the worn mattress.

Fuck! I thought to myself. Now what?

The next few months were hard. My baby was locked up forty seven miles away, in the Oregon State Prison in Salem Oregon. In a way we were both locked up. Prison frustrates the natural emotions of a love now untouchable, nothing but loneliness, and the counting of time, not knowing, only hoping for a quick end to being away from each other. Doing time is not only the sentence of the prisoner but is the sentence of their loved ones, too.

If there was any value to Artent's imprisonment for me, it was to force *me* to re-evaluate my own life and that happened pretty quickly. I came to realize that if she and I were ever to have a real life together, it couldn't be the "fast life." It had to be a more normal Mom and Pop, father goes to work and mother keeps the house kind of life.

I wondered if my Minny Mouse could or *would* change.

Just as fast as Artent was whisked off to jail, I decided to jump back into normalcy myself. I stopped selling coke and weed to my friends, some of whom were still working with PPB, cut off my old connections and stopped being a hypocrite. I had only used cocaine with Artent for a little over 10 months but I quit cold turkey! Abrupt change can be a serious challenge, but I knew it was the only way.

I began looking for work and returned to the business I grew up in, before I joined the Navy. I was raised in the restaurant business, as my parents owned and operated *DuPay's Drive-in Restaurant* on McLoughlin Boulevard, and *The Oak Pit* in St. Johns. Both places I'd worked at over the years going back to when I was a teenager and "soda jerk" and even when I was a young patrolman trying to pay the bills on only $105 a week in 1961. That was how I went back to managing a couple of hamburger joints in the *Herfy's* restaurant chain. This included having to deal with high school kids as employees. It gave me a legitimate income, regular working hours and paid enough to cover the apartment rent and the gas to get back and forth to the prison for my weekly visits with Artent.

Visiting Artent in prison was hard on me. Each week I was strip searched before being allowed into the visiting room, a place I had only seen before as a detective. The grapevine at the prison had been informed that I used to be a cop and that I was visiting a convicted prostitute, a thief, and a Black girl on top of that *and* that she was my girlfriend. I was always escorted into a small private room where the smug smiling guard ordered me to strip. I never had anything to hide. I'm not stupid enough to try and smuggle contraband into a prison, but the guard staff never tried to conceal how much they enjoyed putting me through this ritual, every week. It always ended the same way. "Make sure your report states that I was polite and cooperative!" I would say cheerfully, trying to match the same smug smile they were enjoying at my expense. Then they'd smirk and leave the room so I could get dressed.

The visiting room would be filled with visitors first, before the prisoners were admitted. Then they'd file in one at a time, and be seated across from their guest. Once all the seats were filled, the pent up emotions spilled over and Artent and I were allowed to stand up and kiss, and hug briefly. The guards didn't allow heavy tongue kissing, fondling or groping. It was torture for me not to be able to hold Artent tight and crush her breasts against my chest. After kissing her as much as I thought I could get away with, I poked some change in the vending machines and brought her a soda and a candy bar, setting them in front of her. She would smile and whisper, thank you.

Conversations were hard to start with Artent, during this time, because she was so depressed at being locked up. I tried to be light-hearted, but damn...it sure was fucked. It was impossible to be light-hearted and locked up. It felt forced and fake, me trying to cheer her up. Our conversations generally turned to what we would do upon her release. Eventually, I told her I wanted to be with her for the rest of my life and that we needed to get married. She seemed apprehensive at me going straight. And married? I knew I was coming on strong, but I couldn't help myself. I knew she liked her freedom. She'd been married before, at the tender age of only 17, and had felt trapped. I knew talking about marriage might scare her off but I didn't want to lose her, either.

Artent was in a turmoil of her own, for she had never *known* me as a straight person, and she'd always been in the fast life for most of her adult life. She'd look at me sadly, with love in her eyes but a kind of hopelessness. She knew who and what she was and that any real change would be next to impossible. I was the one who couldn't face the truth about Artent or the prospect of a future together.

Artent's early home life had been hard on her, or so she told me. Her mother Opal Rutherford Thomas had died November 3rd of 1974, when Artent was only 23 and I knew losing her mother had been hard on her. She also had a small son that had been taken from her and was being raised by a close relative

Artent Thomas, Jefferson High School, circa 1968.

of her former husband, a Black man named John Moore. Artent and John married in December of 1968, when Artent was only 17, a few months after graduating from Jefferson High School. Later they divorced in December of 1975, four years before I would meet her, so I knew she'd had a full life in the short years she'd been alive.

Though Artent had graduated from Jefferson high school, and had gotten good marks, she had never gone on to college and had few marketable job skills. I could see the prospect of working a straight job and living 'normal' scared the hell out of her.

"What kind of job could I get?" she mused over her soda. "Tending bar maybe?"

"You'll be on parole when you get out of here," I reminded her. "I doubt they'll even let you *smell* alcohol." She looked down at the floor. "I'll just do a little coke, then," she said coyly, looking up at me with mischievous dark eyes. I could see the old sexy energy light up her face again as we looked at each other.

"Honey?" I screwed my face into a small pained grin as I spoke, trying not to be condescending. "They'll piss test you while you're on parole. No coke—no pot—no alcohol. You'll be lucky if they let you smoke cigarettes, baby?" My voice had a slight pleading quality to it and I hated that. "I don't think I can *do* all that," Artent said, squirming in her chair and looking at me, a worried expression on her face. I held her hand, caressing it with my thumb for a long moment across the table, shaking my head slowly. Artent would be hard to change and we *both* knew it.

****

As the prison time wore on, I continued to become a productive and normal working citizen. I re-joined the boyhood church my mother and I had attended for years. Mom was thrilled at my sudden change. I could see the proudness return to her face when she looked at her once wayward son. "You look healthier Donnie!" she told me one day, "now that you're not coked up all the time *and* you've put on some weight." She was right. It's amazing how much better I felt, ditching the powder and just smoking a little pot. After working as a fastfood restaurant manager for a few months, I landed a prestigious job as security chief at a downtown Portland luxury hotel. I was making a lot more money than flipping burgers and chasing high school kids around, getting them to do their work and not goof off, instead.

Working at the hotel, (it was actually the Benson Hotel) being a department head, I had to wear conservative, expensive three piece suits and shiny black *Stacy Adams* shoes to fit in with the fancy clientèle. It was a fun job in a high-end hotel, eating incredible, high quality food. The employee lunch room was generally the place where all the left-over food from catering events for the rich ended up. The perks were great. There I learned to like quiche (what the hell *was* quiche anyway?) exotic cheeses, various species of sauteed mushrooms and raw oysters on the half shell, seasoned with black pepper Mignonette sauce, high quality cuts of excellent steak and other exotic foods. Rich people spent a lot of money at the hotel and they sure as hell ate well.

Famous people stayed at the hotel too, pulling up in limos or parking their tour buses nearby. The hotel was home for movie stars like Merv Griffin, impressionist Rich Little, concert artists like Gladys Knight and the Pips, Victor Borge, Bob Dylan, and Ella Fitzgerald. I saw them all. Sports greats also arrived regularly like Kareem Abdul-Jabar, and Arnold Palmer. And the biggest star with the most "good-ole boy" security was Waylon Jennings. His security guys were big tough looking white dudes, dressed in all black with radios sticking in their back pockets and serious looks on their faces. It was obvious Waylon didn't take any shit while on the road.

Working in this environment made me feel human again, a person of worth with a future and a real life ahead, someone my mother was proud of again. As a cocaine addict, for just under a year, my mother had a right to be ashamed of me. In truth I had been ashamed of myself. Now, she had renewed faith and when she dropped by work for lunch she was all smiles as she stepped up to the front desk and asked for her son, the "Security Chief." And best of all, I was away from the curse of being a cop and the constant negativity and heartache of seeing people at their worst, hurting themselves and each other every single day of the year. Being a cop *and* being a drug using loser were happily far behind me, dust from a dirty past! I was a church member, I had a checking account. I was brand new, and my mother was proud.

For over six months, I shuttled back and forth from Portland to the prison in Salem once a week visiting Minnie Mouse, the butterfly. While I was busy returning to the status of model citizen, as in fully employed, attending bible studies, and keeping a balanced checkbook, Artent was *not* being a model prisoner. She spent several days in "the hole" for "inappropriate sexual contact" with another female inmate, a young Black girl she'd become friends with.

It had cost her. Her good behavior time had been impacted, and further delayed her release date. According to her "matrix," a confusing and complex formula for figuring the actual exit date of a prisoner with a three-year-sentence, she should have been released in nine months. Well, that wasn't going to happen. I was pissed off at her for doing something stupid that kept her locked up longer. "How could you DO that?" I wrote to her in a letter, since she also lost her visiting privileges. "It happens…" she wrote back, "I've been in here too long." *Six* months was too long?

In the next few weeks I could see two problems heading my way. I was having pains on the left side of my groin and the Doctor at Emanuel Hospital was not subtle about it. "You have a developing hernia that has to be operated on. Your gut is starting to stick through the hole in your abdomen wall and that's why it's hurting. It may have been caused by a previous blunt force trauma injury. Perhaps when you were a cop. When a hernia sticks through like that, it's called a strangulated hernia. You could die if it's not fixed, Mr. DuPay."

I wondered how the hernia had happened. Maybe it was that time I'd been jumped by six drunk, angry men, three white, three Black, when I was working undercover at Van's Olympic Room. Maybe *that* had caused the hernia. In about 1963, I'd been beaten up in the parking lot of Van's working undercover Vice with my partner, Danny. I held onto Pam Owens, an underage prostitute after telling her she was under arrest, and I refused to release her after being cornered by the men. The group pushed us both to the ground and started pummeling me. I remembered all the times they'd kicked me in the head, ribs, stomach, lower abdomen, and back, repeatedly, until I thought I was going to pass out. Maybe that was what had caused the hernia.

Damn! Damn! Damn! I hated even the thought of a scalpel and wondered how long I could put it off. The other problem appeared in the form of a letter from the parole board. When Artent finally got out, she would be paroled to me. At first it sounded great...then it dawned on me that I would be the one *responsible* for her actions. The model citizen thing seemed to be backfiring. I looked good enough on paper to be her keeper, but I *knew* Artent. She danced to her own drum. She did her own thing. She was never mean, or loud, or aggressive. She'd just smile, and wander away and do what she wanted to do. She was born in Mississippi and had learned how to be a "lady" as she put it. I knew full well I would not be able to control Artent in any way, least of all in a way that could actually benefit her.

I was just learning how to be responsible for myself again and I wondered vaguely at the thought process of the parole board. Why had they thought it would be a good idea to parole an independent Black woman to a white man who had once been a cop? Devoted boyfriend? Yes. Lover? Yes. Keeper? Wow! I couldn't control Artent before, so how could I control her in the future?

And then my butterfly got into trouble again. The prison operated a co-ed pre-release center where she would spend her last month. I don't know what *idiot* thought it was a good idea to mix, by now, some very horny men and women together in the same place but in the end, it would be a disaster for Artent. She became involved with a male inmate, and was sent back to the general population and back in "the hole" for several weeks. I don't know what his punishment was but I wanted to castrate the bastard. I was damned mad. I was super pissed at everybody.

How in hell could a prison whose job it is to watch people, be so un-observing that two people could just go off and fuck somewhere? So, yeah they got caught. But where? In a broom closet, or a tool shed? Was it only one time or multiple times? Who knows! And Artent, the little two-timer, how could she cheat on me when I loved her so much? And why did I think she would be faithful to me in the first place? Or serious about the "new life" I imagined for us? Was the "new life" I dreamed about real only to me? Would I be destined never to be with Artent?

Jesus! It could be so good now, for the two of us, if *only* Artent would go straight.

I was working in the *now*, living in the *now*, being content in the now and I wanted her to come with me, so we could be happy together. *Could* we be happy or was she just this pretty butterfly I fell in love with, quiet only when captured for a short time but once out in the world, unable to return to the mundane life of the caterpillar? I wanted Artent to be safe, I wanted her to be happy, but I knew it would be a serious challenge getting past her longtime habits and inclinations.

****

The worsening pain in my groin told me that my appointment with the scalpel wielding doctor who wanted to cut open my guts was not far away. "We'll make an incision and sew a patch over the hole in your abdomen and then stitch you back up," the doctor had told me cheerfully.

"Sounds like you're patching a hole in an inner-tube," I complained.

"Sort of, except we are sewing up the hole not gluing a patch over it."

"I always liked the smell of the rubber patching glue, when I fixed the tires on my bike in grade school," I muttered, mostly to myself. "Me too," volunteered the doctor, "and the smell of gasoline. I used to pump gas when I was a kid going to high school." It sounded like the doc was a regular guy and I would probably be safe in his hands. He patted my shoulder when I left his office and told me not to worry.

At the hotel I placed myself on light duty, to prepare for the hernia operation and spent most of my work days sitting at my desk in my private office, doing paperwork and conning the bus-boys to deliver my lunch from the cafeteria. They felt sorry for me and wanted to be "security professionals," someday and were happy to help me in my diminished state.

I was 'old' compared to them, a guy in his forties, though they'd always tell me I didn't, "...look a day over 36." It worked out great because I could relate to these young kids and they liked me. They knew I started out my career in a restaurant busing tables and working as a sodajerk in my parents restaurants, that I'd then worked as a street cop and a police detective, and now look at me! I had a big fancy desk, a private office with a window and a view, a title with my name on the door, some fancy suits and a staff of security officers to boss around. They looked at me as some kind of God. I gave them tips on police work and they brought me my lunch.

During this time though, mostly I stared at the big wall clock hanging over my office door. When I was thinking about the damned operating table, the hands seemed to spin faster, making time whiz by. And when I was thinking about how much more time Artent had on her matrix, the clock hands seemed to move backward making time just drag. How in hell could time be flying by and dragging at the same time? I reached into my desk drawer and felt around for a bottle of aspirin hiding under a pair of scissors I used to trim employee ID cards. I swallowed three with some hot coffee, and waited for the pain to lessen.

The next morning when I arrived at my office there was a letter on my desk from the Oregon State Parole board. The message was short and to the point. Artent Thomas would be released to me, "...any time after 1300 tomorrow. Please arrange for her transportation." I sat down and read the letter over and over trying to figure out the matrix thing. If she gets released tomorrow she will have served 11 months 13 and one half days on a three year sentence. She would be my legal responsibility for over two years. Whew! I was excited, thrilled, apprehensive and downright scared. This was a humongous responsibility and for a long period of time.

Still my love for Artent was strong, but bruised more than I wanted to admit by her sexual encounters with two inmates. Especially this last fiasco with the man. Minnie Mouse's getting caught the first time with another woman seemed to be somehow different. Two women having sex seemed kinda normal in a women's only prison. But fucking a guy? I couldn't erase it from my mind. In our fast life together I knew she had sex with lots of men for cocaine, but that life was over now. I felt stabbed in the back, betrayed somehow. What had she been thinking?

The next morning I gave myself the day off explaining to the General Manager that I had to meet an old sick friend from out of town who needed my help. I never told *anyone* I had a girlfriend and that she was in prison. Like I always had before, I kept my problems to myself.

That morning, I put on a freshly cleaned three piece. It was a dark blue pinstripe suit, and I looked good in it. I paid a busboy at the hotel garage $10.00 to wash and vacuum out the Cadillac. As I got in the car I could see the reflection of my polished black Stacy Adams shoes in the shiny paint job of the big Cad. I was ready, scared but ready. I was dressed sharp in a nice suit, the Cadillac was clean and shiny and I hoped to make a good impression on my long lost girl, my "old lady," my butterfly.

When I reached the release center there were about a dozen people milling around at the top of the stairs next to the front door, also waiting for rides. I slowly nosed the long black Cad in front of three other cars waiting in line and got a disapproving look from the other drivers that said: *Why do you think you can crowd in line?* And my look back said: *Because I'm driving a Cadillac and you're not!*

I left them sitting there and jumped out of the car, opening the passenger door for Artent, and leaving it open, as she stood at the top of the stairs. I ran up the six stairs to meet her and scooped her up and swung her around in my arms. She smiled and giggled as I easily hefted her thin body in my arms. I was the best dressed guy there and I had the coolest car. An impression had been made. They all must have known I was Artent's "old man" as she still called me.

I set her back down on her feet and stood looking down at her. She was the same Artent but something was different. She was smiling but appeared apprehensive and kept looking back over her shoulder, as if she was worried about something or *someone* who might be watching. "No one is gonna come after you now, baby," I said. "We're going home!" She breathed in the fresh air and looked around at her surroundings, taking a deep breath, and giving me another hesitant smile. With her large brown Bambi eyes she looked for all the world like a deer in the headlights, but she was safe now. We were back together and everything would be alright.

After she got in the Cad and I fastened her seatbelt, I walked quickly around to the drivers side, and slid in. I pushed down hard on the gas pedal and peeled out spraying driveway gravel on the lesser cars underscoring their insignificant status and headed straight for Interstate 5, the freeway that would take us home. For a long time there was an awkward silence between us. Neither of us was sure just what to say. She had been in prison for a long time. She kept glancing at me shyly, as I drove, with hesitant smiles on her face, as if she was not sure who I was, or where she was. Our reunion was more awkward than I anticipated.

We were both the same people, and yet we were different. We had been shaped by the long separation, our opposite lifestyles, her living in a jail cell and me working hard but also living the life of Riley with a car, clothes, money and a cushy prestigious job, all legit now.

In her hands, I could see she clutched a large white envelope. "What's that?" I asked. "Rules and regulations," she replied. "Stuff I don't think I'll be able to live by," she continued quietly. I took the envelope from her, tossed it in the back seat, and blurted out the question I had to ask. "So what about this guy you fucked in jail? What's up with *that?*"

I was jealous and hurt and she knew it. "He's just a guy," she replied in her squeaky little girl voice, the voice she used when she was trying to explain why she had been late getting home from the clubs and thought I might be mad. "He was cute and he has a lot of connections, you know, connections for… coke and stuff. We'll need him later on won't we, baby?" her voice trailed off to a faint whisper. I knew she was in turmoil, but I was still hurt.

At a red light, I reached around for the envelope in the back seat, grabbing it and threw it in her lap. "You're on parole!" I shouted, louder than I intended. "That means no dope, no alcohol, and no strange dick! You're my legal *responsibility* now. You have to straighten up and fly right or there'll be hell to pay. You'll be back in a fuckin' jail cell, Artent! And I'll be alone again! We'll *both* be alone again. Is *that* what you want?"

"I don't know what I want anymore," she whispered, looking out the window.

I reached across her and got a bottle of aspirin out of the glovebox and swallowed three without water. "Listen," I continued, "I have to have a hernia operation in a few weeks and I'm going to be in the hospital for a few days. You *have* to be good. You have to drive me to the hospital and you gotta pick me up when I'm released. Understand?"

"Sure, Don," she said, smiling over at me, that impish light in her eyes, returning.

"I want what's best for you, baby, that's all."

"I know, Don."

I reached over and rested my hand on her knee, gradually feeling higher up her thigh, stroking her smooth skin. "You're mine now baby and no arguments, okay?" I said.

"I'm all yours," she said, giving me direct eye contact.

"I've missed you so *much*, Artent!" I said thickly as I stared ahead, gripping the steering wheel.

"I know, baby. I know."

****

Our little studio apartment, in the Paramount Apartments near the Steel Bridge had been my bachelor quarters for the past several months, and was messy from tender, loving neglect. I never seemed to have time to clean it up and frankly I didn't care much how it looked, as I never had company. My mother had come over once to check on me, and as she looked around, she shook her head and mumbled something about me never cleaning my room at home either, when I was a kid.

The bathroom mirror was speckled with little white spots, toothpaste splashes from brushing my teeth and the dingy bathtub ring showed how high I let the water get when soaking my bones after a long day at the Benson. The only towel was tossed on the floor partially covering an empty toilet paper roll. The main room that made up the apartment was equally messy. The pull down Murphy bed was covered with a pile of dirty clothes, yet to be ferried to the basement laundry room.

A pair of Artent's tiny under-panties hung over one of the arms of the only chair in the apartment. I had never moved them, just looked at them every day like the chair was a little shrine. They were something of hers. They stayed where she'd carelessly tossed them, the last time we made love. I never touched them or moved them, I'd just look at the little pink flowers on them and imagine Artent wearing them again one day.

After Artent walked into our old apartment, and was done looking around, I walked up to her and smiled, shoving off all the clothes onto the floor and smoothing out the blue blanket that lay over the mattress covered in a thin white sheet. I put my hands on her shoulders, looking at her, drinking her in, so glad to be back together with her. She was happy we were finally back together too as she stood there, smiling up at me. I pushed her backwards onto the bed, reached down and gently pulled off her panties, tossing them at the other arm of the chair. She giggled as I propped her little butt up by putting a pillow under her pelvis. She spread her legs and with very little foreplay we fucked. It was less about making love and more about getting it over with. I didn't know whose dick had been in her last but I knew whose dick was in her now. It was mine.

After our unceremonious beginning, the bed springs began to squeak as our hunger for each other returned. Artent clung to me, whispering my name over and over, calling me *Daddy* and telling me how much she'd missed me. I pulled her towards me at the same time I pushed my pelvis against her, holding her tightly in my arms. Push-stroke, pull-stroke, take it and like it, and she did. It had been a long time since we had made love and it was at the same time both awkward and natural. God damn, it felt good to be inside her again! I had missed her little body next to mine more than I realized.

"What was his name?" I whispered rolling off her, the intense orgasm being replaced by the aching pain in my groin. I reached down next to the bed and grabbed a clean paper towel, and nestled it between her legs. "It doesn't matter," she said quietly as she pressed her legs together and laid back, stretching. "I've told you, you're the only Daddy who can make me come, remember?"

"The only 'white' Daddy…"

"Don, come on!"

"You cheated, Artent," I said quietly, uselessly. She ignored the comment.

"Does it hurt?" she whispered, changing the subject and placing her delicate, long-fingered hand over the painful spot, stroking it gently, distracting my thinking. "Yeah, it hurts. I never thought I'd be happy to go to surgery but I can't stand this pain much longer."

I didn't push her for the guy's name anymore. It didn't matter. He couldn't get at her. She was home with me, safe with me, and I was the one responsible. After my operation we would settle into a new routine, I hoped. She wouldn't be fucking other guys anymore, we'd get married, maybe even have a baby and buy a little house with a white picket fence, settle into our own version of The American Dream.

****

But if I hoped Artent was going to be good...if I hoped she could return to *my* definition of "normal," or the parole boards' definition, I was wrong. Barely two nights later, we got into a rare argument. She wanted to go out clubbing and get high. She needed to go and "find some good coke," and I wouldn't let her out the apartment door. I would never hit Artent, so all I could do was stand in her way, which I did, standing in the doorway and telling her no, she had to stay with me, she had to stay at home.

Artent was small, and wiry, but she was also strong, and considering the hernia pain I was suffering, I was next to useless.

156

She was 29, while I was a man in my forties, so when I tried to block the doorway, raising my arms up, she surprised me by hitting me over my left eye with a beer bottle that she had hidden behind her back. Glass on bone, the bottle smacked my skull loudly. As I recoiled, in surprise, grabbing my head, Artent pulled away and ran, grabbing her purse on the way out.

I watched as she tore off, running out the apartment door. Her slinky floral-print dress fluttered in her haste, while she hoisted her purse over her shoulder, trying to stay in her high heel shoes. My poor Artent, she never could get the hang of high heel shoes and how to walk in them. I didn't try to stop her. I was exhausted and the blood dripping into my eyes was an epiphany. I watched as she ran down the apartment staircase of our top floor apartment. I stood motionless and listened as she ran out the front door and into the wet, glistening streets of Portland. The clicking of her heels became fainter and fainter, as blood seeped through my fingers and down into the folds of my neck.

I knew as I drove myself to Emanuel Hospital that my little parolee would never change. The ER doctor asked me what happened and I lied, telling him I'd "fallen down" the marble stairs, in front of our apartment security building. He didn't believe me. He must have known the difference between a fall injury to the forehead, and a high velocity wound. It was obvious someone had hit me. It didn't matter, though. I had long ago stopped caring what people thought of me. It took five stitches to sew up the laceration she inflicted with the beer bottle. Stitched, bandaged and shot up with morphine for the considerable pain, the doctor gave me a Valium to go and released me. Fortunately the hospital and our apartment were not far from each other because I barely remember driving home and crawling into the pulldown Murphy bed with the squeaky springs poking through in places.

I was aroused hours later as shafts of daylight crept through the slats in the mini blinds. It was Artent, her key turning in the lock. After she slipped out of her shoes, and stripped, she snuggled into bed beside me. We didn't speak. I just reached for her and cuddled her in my arms. Cuddled next to me, Artent could always make herself so small and again I was surprised at how petite and thin she was. She smelled like a combination of cigarette smoke from the nightclub, a lingering odor of whiskey on her breath, mixed with the wispy floral scent of her favorite perfume. I was comfortable now. Artent was safe in bed with me and I could stop worrying about her. We were together again, falling asleep without a word passing between us.

****

I finally awoke from my Morphine-Valium grogginess to my brown eyed Bambi awake, propped up on her elbow, and watching me. She was stroking my stitched up forehead gently with her hand, telling me how sorry she was that she had hit me. And she meant it. Kissing me gently and clucking her sorry sound with her tongue, I *knew* Artent loved me. It was in her eyes and in her caress and in every part of her soft body. At the same time I also realized she would never be tamed either by me, the parole board or anyone else. "Baby," she purred, still stroking my head, "I know you have to go into the hospital tomorrow, so I have a surprise for you."

"A surprise?"

"Yeah! We're gonna go to dinner tonight. It'll be someplace nice, like Henry Theile's or any place you like."

"Well, okay. But I'm broke."

"I got it covered. I made some extra last night." I left it at that. I didn't want to know about the extra. Later that night, we had dinner at Henry Theile's in NW Portland. People were surprised to see a decent looking white man in his forties with a much younger beautiful Black girl, but they didn't do or say anything rude and served us our dinner as if we were just like everyone else. I had the prime rib dinner with garlic toast, and Artent had pasta and steak.

As we sat eating, the silence between us was comfortable, like it always was. She kept looking around, taking in the decor, and nibbling at her food, excited to be in a restaurant she'd never been in before. She looked wonderful in a low cut, light blue dress with white lace trim, and a black onyx bead choker and I was so proud to be with her. She was a stunner and when she walked into the restaurant, heads turned.

As I sat there, eating, watching her, I was reminded of another fight we got into shortly after we started seeing each other. I wanted to know why Artent had to see other guys and it was hard to disguise my jealousy. We fought and after yelling that I was cramping her style, she slapped me hard across the face, and stormed off. I ran after her, trying to make it right, but she was gone, like a gazelle. When I ran outside, I could see she was already a block down the street, jogging barefoot with her heels in her right hand and I knew I'd never be able to catch up to her.

She came back late that night, too, with a surprise. It was November of 1977 and the Commodores were in town. I was the last person to know this but Artent always seemed to know what was happening in the Portland music scene, ahead of everyone else.

"We're going to the Commodores concert at the Coliseum tonight!" she told me, as she breezed into the apartment, our drama from only a few hours ago, forgotten.

"Honey, tickets to that are gonna cost at least $50 bucks apiece, and I don't have it, now.

"Got it covered, honey!" She smiled her sexiest smile at me. "Got it covered. All I have to do is show up at the west wing back door and smile at the security guard I met last night at Gatsby's." I was suspicious. "What'd ya have to do fer *that?*" I asked, not wanting to hear the answer. "Don't ask," she replied and I didn't press any further. "We'll get in. All we have to do is show up at 7:30 tonight." I reached up to rub my cheek. "Can you get me an aspirin?" I begged, "I have a headache." Her big dark eyes looked stricken. "I'm sorry. I'm so sorry," she said with real remorse. "It's okay baby," I replied. "I know you didn't mean it."

****

Before we left to see Lionel Richie and the Commodores I fortified myself with a few shots of whiskey. I was determined to have fun and enjoy some good music from one of the hottest groups playing at the time, but I was nervous. What if she left with another guy, like she'd done before? I didn't know what I might do. When we appeared at the back door of the Coliseum the uniformed security officer gave Artent a wink and a smile. She passed him something which he stuck in his shirt pocket after surreptitiously looking around to be sure no one saw. "What was that?" I asked. "A little coke and two Valiums," she said, smiling as we continued walking forward. Not a bad price for admittance I thought and gave her a pat on the butt, happy and excited to be going to a concert with her.

"...And a blow job last night at the club!"

"What?"

"I finished him off with my hand!" she said breezily, as if that made it better.

Jesus, I didn't want to hear that. This girl was crazy, but I loved her. She continued on and I followed. The guard opened the backdoor and we found ourselves at the rear of the hall in a property room storage area where they piled extra risers and folding chairs and other kinds of scenery props and equipment. From there we had to work our way through the gathering crowd toward the front stage area. Artent pushed, wiggled, squeezed and smiled her way, with me in tow to the very front of the stage. Once ensconced, we had a hard time maintaining our position as everyone else was pushing closer, jostling and shoving.

Artent removed one high heeled shoe and held it in her right hand using it as a sort of "space maintainer" to give us room. People looked at her like she was crazy, and I pretended not to notice. Artent was my girl and she could do no wrong. She could also be surprisingly protective of me at times and it touched my heart to witness that side of her, considering how small and skinny she was. Though she didn't look tough, she *was* surprisingly capable.

Once the lights went down, the off stage fog machines began blowing in the atmospheric smoke. It looked like smoke but thankfully didn't *smell* like it. The front edge of the smoke cloud drifted off the leading edge of the stage and out onto the crowd. And with people jumping up and down it looked for all the world like people's heads bobbing up above the clouds and then disappearing, only to reappear again. The ambiance was surreal and otherworldly.

The Commodores rushed onto the stage and started the concert with the song "Brick House." I wrapped my arms around my own little "brick house," and we swayed to the music, blasting beautifully at us from the speakers on the stage. Lionel Richie and the other members dazzled us, dressed in their white out-fits covered in shimmering sequins.

Every movement of Lionel seemed to blend with the music. I could see the lights sparkling and reflecting in Artent's lustrous brown eyes. The next song was *Zoom*, followed by *Machine Gun*. Man, this was so exciting, the music blasting, the crowd yelling and screaming. The intensity was physical. I could feel the sound waves from the base speaker hitting me in the face.

A pair of girls' red panties flew over my head and landed on the stage, followed by a black lace bra. These girls were serious about getting invited backstage to the after party. I couldn't tell which girl they came from though, but all the girls were beau-tiful. They all looked like they wanted a piece of Lionel. The smell of marijuana smoke passed my nose and a white guy I didn't know cheerfully passed me a joint. I took two hits and passed it to Artent. She hit it and soon the joint disappeared into the crowd of other people wanting to smoke it.

The pace of the music went from frenetic to swing and sway when Lionel opened up with his hit song *Easy...easy like Sunday morning.* Artent soaked in the music and the words of the song became her words as she sang along. "*Why does everybody want me to be what they want me to be? I want to be high, oh so high. I wanna be free.*"

Watching Artent in that moment, she became the butterfly again, the butterfly she would always be, the little girl who liked to wander away, be naughty and get lost. By the time the concert ended I knew our relationship might not last and wondered again if Artent would die young. It was something I thought about a lot.

Looking back I could see Artent, the butterfly, would never be able to lead a straight life. She needed to be high and she needed to be free. As we sat in Henry Theile's eating dinner that night, I saw that she would always need to be free. Free of any eight to five, don't-stay-out-late, rules set by the parole board or society in general. Though I loved Artent with all my heart, I could never go back to the fast life. There was no future in it, only chaos and hardship. Prison had only frustrated Artent. She was too young to reflect, as I had. She wasn't done having fun, and taking risks. She was eager to get back to her old way of life, to partying, thrills and getting high.

Prison and almost a year apart had carved our paths in opposite directions.

We didn't speak much the rest of the night, after we got home from dinner. We were both lost in our thoughts. As we eased into bed together I kissed her goodnight and turned my thoughts to the next morning and my impending surgery. I hated even thinking about an operation where they were going to cut open my guts. I fell asleep quickly. Morning would come soon enough.

The pain in my side and in my head where Artent had smacked me with a beer bottle, served as an alarm clock to awaken me the next morning. I tried to make the cobwebs disappear with a cup of instant coffee. I hated instant coffee but it was all we had. The only clean cup I could find was a slightly used Styrofoam cup on the cluttered kitchen counter-top. I hated instant coffee and I particularly hated it out of a Styrofoam cup, as it reminded me of being a cop. But it was that or nothing. I hoped the rest of the day would be better.

We pulled into the hospital parking lot, with Artent driving, she pulled the Cadillac into the short term parking area reserved for unloading patients and parked it there. I hobbled in the front door, looking back so I could see her trailing behind me. "We've been expecting you, Mr. DuPay," said the intake nurse. I was glad they were waiting for me, but I was afraid. Doctors—operating rooms—anesthesiologists, hell what if I died on the operating table?

I gave Artent's hand a tight squeeze, so tight she started to pull back, but stopped, looking at me, concerned. She knew I was frightened. She pulled me to her and looked me in the eye, firmly, like a mother would. "You'll be okay, honey!" she whispered soothingly to me when the nurse wasn't looking. The nurse gave us a curious look because we *were* an odd couple, Artent being Black, and clearly a few years younger than me and me being white, made us stand out. It was something we became used to, as it happened regularly.

I was escorted to my room and told to undress and put on the blue hospital gown laid out on the bed. The nurse disappeared and I put it on. The crazy thing tied in the back, and I could only reach one of the ties. I sat on the bed, testing its softness. The springs weren't poking through so it was better than the Murphy bed at home. The nurse reappeared to see if I was in my gown while Artent slipped a joint into my hand, and then promised to pick me up and take me home in three days.

"It'll be okay, baby," Artent told me. "I'll be back soon, and you'll be FINE!"

"I love you baby! Don't forget about me."

"Never!" she said with a smile and a wave.

Artent laughed, smiling back at me as I stood at the doorway and watched her walk down the hallway toward the exit and my car. Girls' hips just move differently than men and I watched her sexy little butt wiggle into the distance, catching glimpses of the outline of her panties when her thin, slinky, burgundy skirt pulled against her hips. I chuckled when she wobbled, hoisting her leather purse on her right shoulder, and nearly fell out of one of her high heels. That girl never did get the hang of walking in high heels, but God she was beautiful.

I didn't know it then but that was the *last* time I would ever see Artent again.

When Artent disappeared and the nurse was safely gone, I opened the window and smoked the joint. I blew the smoke out of the window, not really caring if the nurse smelled it or not. It relaxed me and after all, if I died on the operating table so what! I climbed into bed and shut my eyes, wiggling around getting comfortable when the nurse reappeared with a cotton swab and a syringe. "What's that?" I asked. "Valium," she replied, sticking me in the arm.

Artent and I had injected a lot of crushed up Valium tablets so I knew what to expect as the warm numbing sensation slowly traveled throughout my body with long determined fingers. I drifted into a half sleep, barely conscious, but aware the bed was moving down the hall toward the operating room. Someone said, "Breathe deeply and count backwards from ten." I remember saying, "Okay, seven, six…" before the lights went out.

After the operation I drifted in and out of my drug induced stupor, unable to move. I could see I had been catheterized. It didn't hurt and I was grateful I didn't have to get out of bed to pee. In fact nothing hurt until the next morning when the nurse removed the catheter telling me I had to get up and walk a little. "Are you kidding lady?" I grouched, "I can't walk. I feel like I've been gutted!" I told her angrily. "Doctor wants you to get up!" she insisted. "You'll get better faster if you start walking." Three days later, after a lot of sleeping and resting in bed, concerned that I hadn't heard from Artent since she left me at the hospital, I sat in the waiting room. I'd been at the hospital three days and I expected her to come and pick me up, and at least call me the day after the surgery.

The nurses were worried I'd been dumped. Did I have a ride they kept asking me? "Is someone coming to get you?" I waited nearly all day and still Artent didn't come. My worry morphed into panic and a sinking feeling in my stomach that something terrible had happened to her, as it hit me like the proverbial ton of bricks that her "girlfriend" could easily have been a boyfriend, instead.

****

After identifying the tortured bloody body of my precious Artent, dumped in a Seattle park, I stayed with my mother for a few days but decided to keep the apartment for another month. I needed time to think, to reflect. Slowly, I reintegrated my life back into working at the hotel, dressing up every day and sleeping without Artent. Portland detectives arrested a Black man at his home about 10 blocks from my apartment and he waived extradition to Seattle. Faced with his bloody fingerprints found in my Cadillac the man confessed to the murder of Artent Thomas.

"But *why!* Why did he murder her?!" I asked the Seattle cop over the phone..

"Well…I think…"

"Was it a drug deal gone bad?" I asked impatiently.

"No, that's not why he killed her. They drove to Seattle together, to get cocaine, but that's not why he killed her."

"Okay?"

"I can read you part of his statement if you want?" the detective said. "Please!" I begged. "You probably won't like this, but here goes." According to the detective, the man had said: "There was no way I was gonna let Artent marry that white *Paddy* motherfucker! Especially if'n he used to be a pig! If I can't have her... *he* can't neether!"

"Who writes a police report in *accent* like that?!" I demanded, suddenly furious.

"He's one of the new guys, some kid from University of Washington, fancies himself a writer."

"That's bullshit!"

"Yeah, I know. So, did you plan on marrying the girl?" asked the detective blandly.

"Yeah, we talked about it," I replied, stunned at this new information. "That crazy bastard killed her because she was gonna *marry* me?!" I demanded, still furious. "A love-triangle killing…" said the detective matter-of-factly. That was it, plain and simple. "I'm sorry for your loss," he concluded before finally hanging up before I could answer back. He sounded exhausted and indifferent, like so many homicide detectives before him. I remembered the feeling well.

As I hung up the phone, I thought back to an afternoon in the early 1970s when me and my buddies in the PPB burglary office watched a depressed man from the Hooper Detox Center across the street jump out a second story window. The man seemed to fly out the window landing head first onto the pavement below, where he was killed instantly.

Mike O'Leary, a cynical old Irish detective who had seen it all was unmoved. He smirked, standing in front of us, as we all crowded together at the window, looking north and said: "Well, looks like Hooper cured another drunk!" I walked back to my desk, listening to the others laugh and go back to their desks when I realized I had felt nothing, too, just like O'Leary. The difference I believe was that it *bothered* me that I felt nothing.

After the trial, which took place quickly, I returned to our little apartment to stay for a while. I was exhausted. My emotions were dead. I couldn't cry anymore. There were no more tears left. I felt numb. Nothing ever seemed to work out for me in the love department, and Artent's murder pushed home that fact.

One afternoon, I pulled down the squeaky Murphy bed where we had slept together so many times, snuggled in each other's arms. I smoked a good sized joint Artent had left behind that I'd failed to notice before. There it was on the kitchen counter, in an ashtray, half smoked but with her signature red lipstick all over the paper. I smoked it down to the nub and then after looking at it for a moment, popped the remaining fragment in my mouth. The fragment was only the smallest bit of paper with her red lipstick all over it and a few bits of marijuana bud inside. I chewed what was left of it, staring vacantly out the kitchen window, and swallowed. It made me feel *closer* to her, somehow. I laid down on the bed, not bothering to undress and turned over, pulling the covers over my head and eventually fell into a fitful half-sleep.

All I could hear was the detective's words over and over like a broken record in my mind and stuck on that one phrase, knowing I had not been there to protect her and that an evil man had taken her life rather than see her happy with me.

"She was stabbed 27 times—She was stabbed 27 times—She was stabbed 27 times."

A couple of weeks later, with the early morning fog hanging outside, I crawled slowly out of bed to get ready for work at the Benson Hotel. I showered, shaved, found my clothes, and put on my suit, slipping into my Wingtip dress shoes. I usually walked to work, going across the Steel Bridge to get to the Benson but this day, I'd be taking my car, the same car Artent drove to Seattle with, and her killer drove back to Portland with, his hands on the steering wheel, the same hands he'd used to kill my Artent with.

I took the car because I knew I wouldn't be coming back to our little apartment ever again. I had already given the manager notice. There was no way I could continue living there. I put my remaining belongings into a large black garbage bag, folding my clothes as best I could and twisting the top into a knot that I could easily grip in my hand. Satisfied there was nothing left to take, I looked around the room, taking it all in, savoring for a moment the little apartment that had been my home with the beautiful and doomed Artent Thomas.

There were many things I left. Her scattered clothing that she'd tossed here and there, her cosmetics and tubes of the bright red lipstick she favored, even a bottle of perfume, Tabu, that I had bought for her as a gift. I couldn't take any of it with me. Artent was lost to me. All I had left were memories of our time together.

I left the key in plain sight on the rumpled bed. I walked silently past the doorway and turned around for one last look, then quietly closed the door behind me, trying not to disturb the still remaining shadows of a sweet dream that could have been, but was destroyed instead with a knife.

Artent Thomas in her early 20s.

Chapter 4

My Friend Katherine and How Heroin Came to Albina

"The wet air was as cold as the ashes of love,"
—Raymond Chandler, author of *Farewell My Lovely*

Kathryn was a beautiful woman in late 1980. She had silky, clear olive skin, shoulder length, straight black hair and fine features, which revealed her Native American heritage. Her mother was a Warm Springs Indian and her father, a tall white man, which was about all she could remember about him. Standing up tall Kathryn stood five feet eight inches. "That's all I got from my father," she would say, "Just my height." Kathryn was pragmatic about her father saying she barely remembered him. "It is what it is," she would say philosophically. "Except I do remember he smelled of tobacco, a lot."

Because of her height and slender figure I felt Kathryn was sexy. Often she would wear loose fitting solid color peasant dresses which would cling to her figure as she moved about. She had an impish beguiling smile, and when she parted her mouth in a flirty smile, she revealed even white teeth. It was her smile that misled me, and threw me off when we first encountered each other years before, outside Van's Olympic Room, in 1963.

At the time I was working the Albina district as a Portland police officer, and only 27-years-old, but more on that later.

Kathryn's previous lifestyle and the fact that she had a 13-year-old daughter named *Shabra,* and was pushing forty allowed for a few "wisdom wrinkles" as she called the creases near her eyes and the smile lines around her mouth. She often searched her temples for any grey hair that was emerging, and I would watch as she plucked them out, joking about how she was getting older. I was not in love with Kathryn, but our relationship was developing and I did have a bit of a crush on her. We were friends, pot smoking buddies, and hung out at the Dekum Tavern at NE Union and Dekum, and over at Sloan's on Vancouver Avenue. This was all during my days in late 1980, which was two years after I had resigned from PPB, having grown tired of the racism, the corruption and the drug dealing that happened in the department on a regular basis and went unchecked.

When Kathryn and I spent time together, we would hold hands, sip beers and try to play pool, though neither one of us was very good at it. I was never much interested in playing pool or hanging about in taverns but I wanted to be around Kathryn and that was always where she wanted to go.

I felt Kathryn was showing me off to her acquaintances and friends in the taverns we frequented, because she seemed to be proud to be seen with me. I could definitely tell and it was flattering. Her daughter's father had been a black man and I could tell why he had loved her. Kathryn was beautiful, pale-skinned and biracial, but I always felt that way—that she was showing me off, perhaps because I was a white man, or maybe just because she thought I was good looking—I never did quite figure that part out.

Although we came from wildly different backgrounds, Kathryn was the significant other and one time girlfriend of one LeRoy Clarke, an old nemesis of mine. LeRoy was the premier heroin dealer of the early 1960s in the Albina district, (where I had been working as a young police officer) and yet despite our past, Kathryn and I were still drawn to each other when we ran into each other in 1980.

After we reconnected, bumping into each other at *Sloane's* one night, we were drawn together for another more complex reason. Besides our obvious attraction to each other, we had each suffered the loss of our partners, both of whom had been Black. My fiancé, Artent Thomas, had been horribly murdered in Seattle by a former boyfriend in May of 1980 at the age of only 29, stabbed 27 times and beaten nearly beyond recognition. And LeRoy Clark was killed in a shootout with the PPB SWAT team in Van's Olympic Room in 1977 three years before I would lose Artent, who I often called my "beautiful butterfly."

The trauma and loss Kathryn and I experienced was the magnet that pulled us together. We both knew what had happened to each other, having heard it through the Portland grapevine. But to get some backstory, you'll need to return with me to the long ago time of the Albina of the 1960's. I understand most people reading this will have not lived during that time, nor have any awareness of just how bad it was in Albina then, but you can take my word for it, it was bad.

The Albina district was nothing like the Albina of today with all the new apartments and condos, coffee shops, fashion boutiques, bike lanes and pizza parlors. Albina in the 1960s was a lawless heroin and alcohol fueled shoot 'em up, Wild Wild West show, with blood running into the sidewalk cracks from almost weekly shootings, and regular knifings.

There was run-of-the-mill chaos occurring nightly in the many clubs. Mostly they were rundown dumps filled with every kind of vice you could think of. The carnage happened regularly in front of *King's Tavern* on Williams Avenue or *The Red Sands* at Union and Shaver or another lawless tavern, which never had a name, located at NE 15th and Prescott, and which was rather similar to a "blind pig." A blind pig is a term for a nameless, illegal drinking establishment not registered or licensed with the city.

Heroin was as available in Albina as *Prince Albert Crimp Cut* smoking tobacco, and *Zig Zag* rolling papers were also available. In short, Albina was a dangerous ghetto, edgy in the daylight hours and downright dangerous once the sun went down, especially if you were a white person walking alone. After dark, that was when the predators came out, searching for victims to mug, rape, knife and rip off in any way they could, from stealing their shoes, to their jacket or purse, to their wallet or car.

My first introduction to Albina was in 1961 as a young and naive probationary cop. I spent three months working the area with my first coaches. We checked most of the watering holes. Mainly my coaches liked stopping at Van's Olympic Room at North Vancouver and Fremont.

The old building has been torn down and in its place is a large condominium. The area where Van's Olympic Room sat is now an open air common area, between the two buildings, with plants, shrubs and an attractive walkway with decorative rocks.

Van's was a small boxy building that was located north, a considerable distance from the edge of Fremont street, resting in the middle of the block. There was lots of space for parking all around the club, and it was always crowded. Drinks were served freely to anyone old enough to sit up straight on the bar stool or hide in a back corner table, this included teenagers who were clearly underage.

When we walked in, and found a place to sit, no one seemed to take notice of the two uniformed police officers drinking coffee at the bar. Attractive black women rotated, dancing on top of a grand piano. They were stripped down to a G-string and had pasties covering their pert nipples. LeRoy Clarke managed the club. He was a "smooth" light skinned Black man about six feet tall and quite good looking. Women called LeRoy "pretty" and his rare smile showed perfectly straight, white, cared for teeth. LeRoy tended the bar and watched the goings on around him, usually with a serious expression, and a downturned mouth and furrowed brow.

It seemed LeRoy was always troubled, with something on his mind. When he bent down to reach for a clean shot glass from the lower shelf, I could see the outline of a snub nosed pistol tucked in the back pocket of his spotlessly clean pressed grey slacks.

The club was owned by a white man in his middle fifties, a man with the unlikely name of *Elwin Van Riper*, hence, *Van's Olympic Room*. Van always sat at the very end of the bar with his highball glass kept full by LeRoy. He watched the crowd but mostly he watched the beautiful black strippers as they danced on the piano top, wiggling seductively. With jet black hair from a dye bottle, which was greased straight back and sporting a pencil thin mustache, Van reminded me of the 1950s TV detective character Boston Blackie.

Illustration by Truxton Meadows.

While I too enjoyed watching the crowd *and* the exotic strippers wiggle and shake, I wondered why my coach and partner never said *anything* about the underage drinking that was occurring right under our noses. I also wondered why we never stopped the shiny Cadillac's driven by pimps or talked to the hookers soliciting customers on Union Avenue, most of whom were young black girls.

I was on probation, a rookie then, and knew enough to keep my mouth shut about what went on. As the cops on the district, we answered calls, but rarely did anything proactive by today's standards. It was a completely different time then, which many people criticize today. But one can't judge people who lived and worked sixty years ago with the moral standards of *today*. There is no way people of today can understand the pressure we were under then, unless they were there themselves working alongside us and *alive* in the 1960s.

The truth was that Albina was a lawless free-for-all where anything went. I learned the police looked the other way when it came to many petty crimes occurring in Albina. Things like rape, and murder and child molestation they investigated, but many other vice crimes were swept under the rug. This surprised me as a young recruit, because I thought we were supposed to go out and "fight crime" rather than allow it to go on unhindered or unchallenged. The underage girls, the drinking and hooking, all of them pretty Black girls, it bothered me a lot. Where were their parents? Why didn't anyone *care* that they were just kids being led astray?

The Vice Squad

It wasn't until I was assigned to the Vice Squad that I figured out how the heroin business was operated in Albina and *who* was running it. Heroin had been in Portland for decades before I was hired on with the department in April of 1961 and in fact had been circulating in Portland since before I was born. What I had always heard from my superiors at PPB was that heroin was shipped in from *China* and had been since the turn of the century. The Chinese in Portland, got it directly from China, from family and friends, and then supplied it to the Black people living in Albina over in the North End.

Originally, it was opium that came from China in the late 1800s, winding up in the notorious opium dens that were active in Portland during the early 1900s. Chinese heroin came to many other places, too, like Seattle, San Francisco and NY. The opium from China arrived in Portland for Chinese use around the turn of the century, and in time other ethnic groups began to use it, and it wound up firmly entrenched in the Black communities in Portland. Heroin is a derivative of opium and it didn't take long before heroin was the drug of choice for many people living in the North End.

In recent years there is a growing myth among certain newcomers to Portland that "white men" brought heroin to the Black community in Portland, in an effort to sabotage Black folks. That is simply not true. Neither is it what I heard from my superiors with PPB, and that is not what I witnessed during my time working for PPB. That myth has been debunked by the history that has been recorded.

Opium and then heroin, coming to Portland, came from *China.*

Vice was always looking for new guys for undercover operations, young cops still fresh faced, eager and idealistic enough to do the job, and I guess I fit the bill. I was seasoned but was still ambitious, and still young enough to be suitably naive, and so I transferred to the Vice Squad on December 27, 1962 two days after Christmas.

The change from uniform to plain clothes was a challenge for me. The first challenge was the working hours, from eight p.m. to four a.m. Hanging around the house waiting until nearly eight o'clock, at which time I would go to work, made me feel restless. I was anxious to get downtown and get to work. I loved being a police officer. Feeling that I was doing something useful for the city I grew up in and came of age in, making Portland safe, solving problems and restoring peace and order was an intoxicating feeling. It made me feel important and that I was on the side of *good* and was of service to the Portland community.

I was young, an idealist and in many ways, gullible.

After a long dinner with my first wife, a few minutes past six pm I'd jump into the car and get to work. Parking downtown by the police station was easy as the parking meters were no longer operating, and there were available vacant spots.

The second challenge was working in blue jeans and a casual shirt and jacket. Only *you* know you're a cop on duty when you're working Vice. You come to realize how much work the uniform actually does *for* you and the transition was hard. I didn't like it. I didn't like pretending I *wasn't* a police officer. I was proud to be working for PPB and I didn't like pretending I was a regular Joe and not the police officer that I was.

The Vice office was a windowless room on the second floor of the old Police Headquarters building, big enough for four big desks and a blackboard on the largest wall. The walls were painted a light institutional green and the wall just inside the door sported four clipboards containing reports from the "uniform cars" on suspicious activity in their districts. We always looked over the reports to see if there might be a problem we could help with when we went on patrol.

The boss in Vice was Lt. Jack Strudgeon, a nefarious figure with his fingers regularly in the pie, so to speak. Of course I didn't know that at the time, being a green rookie. My partner was Officer Danny Stohl, a seasoned cop with over ten years on, tired of the uniform and like me, straight as an arrow. Well, as straight as you *could* be working Vice and doing illegal things (like drink on duty and drive drunk) in the process of trying to perform your job. Lt. Strudgeon would give us both twenty dollars in "drinking money," to get the night started with the promise of more cash if we ran into a situation which required some "front money" for something more complicated, like drugs or a prostitute.

Illustration by Truxton Meadows.

On the blackboard was a flowchart of the who's who in the Portland heroin trade. At the top of the chart was Mr. Way Lee, a Chinese man and longstanding Portland drug dealer. Below

Lee were several of his Lieutenants and at the bottom of the chart were some low-level known heroin dealers, all Black. They included men like Sherman Jackson, Henry Johnson, and Herman "Candy" Canyon and other down-line dealers. Among other names were Jaynolen Moody, Buck Owens (no relation to the musician of the same name) and of course, Le-Roy Clarke. It was no secret to the police who the heroin traders were in Portland. It was well known, in fact.

Danny and I had an unmarked car. It was a 1957 Ford, two-tone, pale green and white. In the back seat was a baby safety chair, numerous ratty teddy bears, a pink plastic play telephone, and other kiddie toys. The radio to dispatch was hidden in the glovebox and an old windup siren was located under the hood of the car. There was a button on the floor to activate the siren if we ever needed to stop a car. The unmarked car looked like my family car, or perhaps the car of a single mother.

Our assignments were to park the car, and hit the bars. Most of them were located off West Burnside Street, and in other areas in the city now known as China Town. We were told to look for prostitutes or "find a whorehouse to harass" by talking to any John's trying to locate a hooker for sex. We were regularly told we should tow John's cars that may or may not have been parked "over a foot from the curb" as the John's were trying to leave and go home from a night out drinking. *Anything* to either arrest them or have their cars towed, we were told by our superiors.

In the bars we would buy a drink and watch the crowd looking for something to get involved in or for someone we could easily bust. This brought up the third challenge, being *paid* to drink and then *drive* an unmarked police car and hoping we wouldn't get "burned" over time. In other words we hoped the regulars wouldn't figure out we were actually cops by seeing our faces often enough.

The ultimate challenge of Vice continued for me. One week I'm in uniform arresting people for drinking and driving, feeling good about myself and now I'm the one drinking and driving and worse yet, pretending I *wasn't* a cop. It was confusing, disconcerting and worrisome. It felt like I was lying and I *didn't* like it.

What if I was in an accident while I had been drinking? We never talked about that, and our lieutenants never once brought it up. They would tell us only: "*You have to be okay with the drinking. You gotta be okay with it.*" The pressure to go along was tremendous. No one wanted to admit he couldn't "be a man" and drink as part of our cover. This led to more than a few accidents happening with other officers, though no accidents happened while I was behind the wheel.

After a few weeks getting oriented to the duties of a Vice officer chasing whores and harassing gay people, (which I didn't enjoy doing and did not believe was right in any way) I decided to concentrate my time in Albina. I wanted to see if by watching the heroin trade in action, anything could be done about it. I'd already witnessed, as a patrolman working the streets, the destruction that heroin addiction brings, particularly to the women and *girls* who would do anything to get more of it. They invariably wound up under some pimps sadistic thumb, and clenched fist. The plight of young confused prostitutes bothered me a lot.

I was quite cognizant of the fact that our Mayor at the time, Terry Shrunk, had barely escaped the wrath of the McClellan Commission Hearings in Washington DC, which occurred in early 1957. Their purpose was to investigate crime and corruption in Portland. Portland had become notorious for a time during the late 1950s and many people in Portland were embarrassed about it.

Chief of Police Jim Purcell Junior was indicted August 3, 1956 for "Incompetence, delinquency and malfeasance, for failing to suppress illegal gambling, boot legging and prostitution," within Portland, which he claimed to *love*. I knew that Schrunk was as corrupt as any dirty cop and perhaps even more so, and everyone *else* knew it, too. Within the Portland Police Bureau and elsewhere. Slippery "Diamond Jim," was not convicted of any crime as a result of the 1957 investigation, but he *was* as crooked as ever. This, even after he was indicted and found to be operating *two* whorehouses located in Albina while he was working as Captain of North Precinct. Purcell's criminal activity was occurring of course at the same time that the McClellan Commission was conducting their investigation.

With Shrunk as Mayor of Portland, and Jim Purcell as Captain of all of Albina, both of them corrupt to the marrow, I was operating in an impossibly untenable and stressful situation. I was trying to fight crime, but was surrounded by it within the political and administrative structure of PPB. This was the early 1960s in Portland and it was a very different time. I was a young idealistic cop trying to make the world a better place, and fight crime and corruption for the good working citizens of Portland, who were both white *and* Black, but the crime and corruption was so deeply embedded within the command staff that it took me a while to figure that out.

Lt. Strudgeon, when I first started working under him, never mentioned *any* of these facts to me. But then why would he? He just gave us our "drinking money," and told us to stay out of trouble, whatever *that* meant and then disappeared within the dim corners of Bill's Gold Coin, which was a well-known gangster hangout on West Burnside Street. The girls at Bill's were plentiful, attractive and available and I'm sure he had a good time. There Strudgeon would sit at the bar, drink and watch everyone. Billy Moe, the owner, was routinely being investigated for running girls and fencing stolen items, but Moe always seemed to be one step ahead of the law and he continued to evade justice for a long time. Clearly, he was protected by some of the powerful men within the command structure of PPB.

There were several nightclubs and taverns on NE Williams Avenue, *The Cotton Club*, and *Paul's Paradise Club*, were both owned by successful businessman, Paul Knauls Sr. There was the *Texas Playhouse*, and *Kings Tavern*. *Van's Olympic Room* was on North Vancouver Avenue and Fremont, and the *Paragon Club* was located on NE Killingsworth and Vancouver, with *The Red Sands* on NE Union and Shaver. They were trouble spots of every kind of vice.

All of these establishments were located within a mile of each other and were outlets for heroin, and pills. This included, uppers, downers, and liquor by the drink or by the bottle. All of the aforementioned substances were available for anyone who had the cash and could still manage to successfully navigate sitting upright on a bar stool. As incredible as this must sound to modern day readers, no employees or managers in these places *ever* checked ID. It just wasn't done in those days. The club owners didn't *care* how young some girl was, they just wanted the business, the money. They didn't care if girls got raped in the parking lots, or manipulated into becoming prostitutes by the parasite pimps who were lurking in every dark corner. They were selling their "get highs" and the fast-life crowd was buying.

When I started out, I found myself beginning my evening work as a vice officer generally at The Cotton Club. It was the first club in the string of clubs on Williams Avenue, and after a few weeks of observing the fast crowd it seemed to be where the nightly action always began.

I was usually the only white guy in the place and I'm sure they figured out I was not there shopping for smack or a romp in the hay with one of their beautiful available women. I would go in, buy a Black Velvet whisky with a water back, and find a table near the stage. From that vantage point, I could see the front door and who would be coming and going. While I drank and watched the girls dance, I became adept at maintaining a perfect poker face. You had to. It meant your survival.

It was never my intention to make an arrest in the Cotton Club as I would have been mobbed if I'd ever tried to, but to just find out what was going on and who the important players were. I was there to eavesdrop, watch people and gather information. In time, I began to recognize the faces of the various heroin dealers, the ones listed on the blackboard in the Vice office. For example, Jaynolen Moody would park his shiny black Cadillac in front of the Cotton Club, for all to see and make a grand entrance into the club, swaggering nonchalantly, slapping his buddies on the back, flirting with the women, and acting like a bigshot.

Illustration by Truxton Meadows.

On his arm he generally had his main squeeze, Thelma Moody, leading the way in one of her revealing skin-tight black satin dresses, with black pumps and black stockings. Thelma was a stunner, 20-years-old and a heroin junkie. She wore a lot of bright red lipstick and always smelled of seductive *Tabu* perfume, which was known to be popular among Black women. When she walked in, all the men turned to look at her. I noted Jaynolen and Thelma's vital statistics in my field notebook as surreptitiously as possible as I sipped my whiskey, blending in with the mostly working class crowd.

I needed to get a copy of their mug shots for my file, which I kept in the backseat of my undercover car, hidden under some teddy bears and a baby blanket. As I had a visual of them and knew exactly what they looked like, I would need their mug shots for later on, in case I needed to positively identify them.

The pimp, Buck Owens, would also show up nightly at the Cotton Club, with his junkie girlfriend and prostitute, 19-year-old Pam Owens. Both Pam and Thelma went by their pimps last names, which was common at the time. Candy Canyon would arrive around the same time, parking his shiny black Cadillac in front on the street. Sherman Jackson who drove a blue Rolls Royce would come to the Cotton Club on a regular basis, as well.

And of course there was the loudly dressed and the most unmistakable pimp and drug dealer of all who showed up regularly, and that was the well-known Henry Johnson. Johnson was always trying to attract as much attention as possible with his absurd purple and lavender suits and his smug, defiant attitude. He was a pimp and he was proud of his vocation, and "fuck you" if you didn't approve. That was his attitude. Johnson didn't care that he was a blood sucking parasite, living off of women because he had no skills, talent or work ethic, he genuinely thought he looked good in his cheap, tasteless suits.

At the Cotton Club, and generally looking their best, these folks would acknowledge each other, stopping to chat, and share a drink, eyeing each other, commenting on their new threads. The flashy cars and 'Look At Me' clothes were the visible shells of excess these folks thought were important. The other reality was that at home they often slept on mattresses on the floor with no bedding other than ratty old woolen blankets. They often sat on apple boxes or the dusty floor with only a sofa cushion or pillow to support their behind. In their empty houses they would eat potato chips, onion dip and drink Kool Aid from a cable reel they used as a tabletop.

Their clothing was always bright and eye-catching, and their cars gleamed, but their homes were pathetic examples of life-long poverty and not knowing how to even *make* a home. They didn't know how to buy furniture, paint a wall or fix a leaking sink. They only knew how to dress the part of a winner, as if they were donning a costume, but they didn't actually know how to *be* a winner.

It was obvious that the Cotton Club was where the Black in-crowd gathered to begin their work night and show off their badass rides and threads. In time I began to see that the Cotton Club was where these characters picked up their heroin packages for the night, to sell and surreptitiously to use. I later added more of these characters to my back seat mugshot file. I would request office printouts of each of their rap sheets from the secretaries at the police station so I could study them and become familiar with the criminal histories connected to each face. Like many police officers, I became very good at remembering faces.

Stopping by *Paul's Paradise Club* to watch the crowd and have a beer was generally my next stop of the night, when working Vice. Paul's Paradise Club was just a few blocks from the Cotton Club on Williams and Russell. "Paul's Paradise" as we used to call it was more like *Paradise Lost*. It was less classy than the Cotton Club and had a more common *tavern* atmosphere.

Still, there were pretty young Black girls sitting at the end of the bar, all waiting to get picked up and prostituted for money. And they were *all* underage. When I walked in and sat down at the bar, the girls would give me the eye, and try to flirt, thinking I was a working class white man looking for a good time with a "colored" girl. I waved them off by acting disinterested, and pretended to concentrate on my drink, looking glum and depressed as I stared down into my glass of frothy beer.

But the undertone and the intensity of *other* things for sale was barely disguised by the innocent tunes emanating from the tinkling jukebox. Songs like "Big Girls Don't Cry" by the Four

Illustration by Truxton Meadows.

Seasons and "The Locomotion," by Little Eva and the occasional whiff of marijuana smoke added to the edgy ambiance and sense of danger. This was the 1960s and marijuana was considered a "hard drug." I was always on alert when I went to Paul's Paradise for these reasons because you never knew what might happen.

Williams and Russell was the "Hollywood and Vine," of the Albina ghetto in those years during the 1960s, and known as "the Avenue" by all police. The strip had more taverns and bars, including Sloan's, which had the frontend of a semi truck decorating the Vancouver side of the building.

There was a hip clothing store, called *Lew's Men's Shop*. The owner, Lew, was a white man who sold flashy suits of all colors with satin dress shirts to match and bright green neckties along with a line of shiny, high quality, Stacy Adams shoes. His clientele were the Black men of Albina, both the crooks and the honest working class, with the money to burn to look good.

Williams and Russell was the place to *see* and be *seen*, with folks hanging out in front of the taverns smoking and drinking beers or sneaking a swig from a pint in their back pocket, yelling at friends across the street and waving at people driving by in cars. Often if I stopped to listen outside a bar, blending into the darkness, I could hear the men talking shit about each other's mothers. They called these contests, "the dozens." They would start out with *Yo Mama Fat jokes*: "Yo mama so fat, her picture keep fallin' off the wall!" or "Yo mama musta whupped you wit da ugly stick, yo so *uu-glee!*" or "Yo mama so ugly she halfta sneak up on a glass of water tuh git a drink!"

Illustration by Truxton Meadows.

The men would laugh, slap their thighs and sneak another drink from a flask hidden in their jackets. In some ways I felt privileged to glimpse their intimate yet casual nightlife customs, something not common for most white people hanging out in the ghetto late at night. I found much of their laughter and fun loving nature appealing. It was the flip side of the relentless addiction their lifestyles also allowed that showed me that most of them were doing the best they could with what they had been given in life.

If you stood in front of the Paradise Club you could throw a beer bottle across Williams and hit the front entrance of The Texas Playhouse, that's how close they were to each other. I never spent much time checking out "the Playhouse '' as it was called. It was just a rerun of the other watering holes on the strip, and I knew most of the regulars who went there. The same group of hookers and pimps rotated through these businesses looking for customers on a nightly basis. It was a chaotic merry-go-round of madness, loud music, drunkenness, scoring dope and making connections for later on—always with a wink or a nod.

One night that I remember vividly, I parked the Ford with the teddy bears in the back a couple blocks away on North Vancouver and walked to the front door of Van's Olympic Room. Thelma Moody, whom I had already seen earlier that night at the Cotton Club was dancing on the grand piano at Van's. I ordered a Black Velvet in a bucket glass with a splash of soda from LeRoy Clarke who was tending bar. He nodded his head at me in acknowledgement, but was not friendly.

I was *certain* LeRoy recognized me, from when I went to Van's while I was a probationary rookie with my training coach, Officer Fred Brock. *No matter, he knows me, so what*, I thought. *I'm just here watching the business.* LeRoy was one of the most reserved Black men I ever came across. He rarely spoke. He would look up from leaning over and polishing the bar glasses and scan the crowd. He was highly alert and I could tell also *highly* intelligent. I often wondered what he was looking for as he scanned the crowd at Van's. His troubled brow told me he rarely had the luxury of ever being able to relax or coast. It was clear his life was constant stress.

LeRoy was watching for something, maybe a familiar face, or maybe he was just worried about any potential trouble. That night I ignored him for the moment and worked my way to the back wall. I remembered LeRoy always had a gun stuffed in his back pocket but I had a gun, too. As I scanned the crowd I wondered who else had guns. I found a small table and sat down to watch the crowd. The club was packed.

Plus the ten bar stools they had, there were about twenty cocktail tables with two or three people at each table. Most people were talking and drinking, laughing and smiling, and a few were obviously under the drinking age but it wasn't my job to check IDs that night.

Some patrons were watching Thelma wiggle, mostly the men of course. And Thelma *was* beautiful. She had long brown legs, a thong tucked into her butt cheeks and pasties covering her nipples. As I watched her dance I noticed she was repeating the same fluid movements over and over as if her body was on a taped loop. Her smile was showing through the thick red lipstick she wore, but the smile was unmoving as if she was a mannequin stuck with one expression and the repetitive motions of a machine.

Thelma was high. *Very* high.

She was dancing because she was supposed to—and smiling for the same reason. Dancing for bills customers would stick in her G-string, dancing to kill time until she would pick the most desirable John to meet after work and go with him to prostitute herself for more money in her little dump of a house that she rented. The heroin made the pain of doing what Thelma had to do a little easier, if you worked as a Go-Go dancer/hooker in 1960s Portland. The heroin made it a little easier to mask your loss of self respect, a little easier to hide your shame behind a frozen plastic smile, and a little easier to forget.

Most of these girls, like Thelma, and Pam were raised in religious Christian households and yet they had fallen to the wayside. They had been lured into "the life" and were doing things they didn't feel good about. They were stripping and hooking, and the heroin made it easier to sin against the Jesus their mothers and aunties often lectured them about.

Another night, Jaynolen Moody dropped Thelma off to go to work. Her shift was just starting. This was business and I knew he would go on to peddle his wares elsewhere, at a different club. In my mind I can see the taillights of his Cadillac disappear up Fremont Street with another doomed young woman sitting beside him listening to his lies and empty promises of the good life, if only she would have sex with yet another man and give *him* the money afterwards.

During the recruitment phase of getting girls to prostitute, a pimp like Jaynolen might shower a girl with affection and gifts, *and* lies, particularly if she came from a good family and was lightskinned, because Black pimps *always* preferred the lightskinned girls.

"You wanna go to the top doncha, baby?"

"We're gonna have the good life, I promise, just me and you!"

"You're my number one girl, you just gotta keep doin' this fer a while."

"I need you, baby. No one can do what *you* can."

"Okay, Daddy–yeah, Daddy–sho thing Daddy," was often what these girls would say in response. It would take years for the lucky ones to wise up, because most of them didn't wise up. Most of them wound up dead.

That's what pimps would say at first in the beginning, when they were trying to come across like Romeo Pimps, those pimps who could use psychological manipulation to control prostitutes. After a few months or maybe only a few weeks, pimps would drop all pretense of their favorite girl getting to the "top" or having the "good life" and their attitude would change and threats replaced the sweet talk.

At that point, the pimps would control their stable almost entirely by threats of violence, beatings, and force. This could include cutting. Pimps would cut a girl in a place where it might not show, like the inside of her thigh, or in the crease of a buttock. This served the purpose of showing the girl he could kill her if he wanted to, and that he was not unwilling to cut her if she didn't hand over all the money she earned. He wouldn't destroy her face, but rather cut her where it wouldn't show.

However, there were also vicious pimps who *would* destroy a girl's face and particularly if they were getting older, or were not very pretty in the first place, or were known as Lot Lizards, hookers who were being sold at truck stops and the like. I came across girls who had their faces beaten in and knew they would never look the same. The terror of their pimps was something you could not get past as a police officer. They would not budge and I could *never* get them to talk.

The night when Thelma had finished dancing her set, with her drugged and plastic smile, and the taped music had stopped blasting over the speakers, she eased herself down from the piano top and sat on the very end stool of the bar. LeRoy walked over and silently filled a tall glass with some kind of hard liquor, mixed with Coke and placed it on the bar in front of her. At first she sipped from the straw that was in the drink, but then she quickly removed the straw and tossed it on the bar top and swigged the rest of the drink down in one long gulp, blocking the ice cubes with her nice straight teeth. Thelma had cotton-mouth. She was thirsty.

I finished my drink and stood up slightly unsteadily on my feet. I worked my way between tables to the front door. LeRoy was watching me, and nodded to me as I headed my way to the door, glad to see me leaving no doubt. Outside smelled like a fragrant elixir of springtime Portland air compared to the smoky, close, unhealthy atmosphere inside Van's.

I waited outside the front door until I'd taken four or five deep breaths of fresh air. Then I straightened up and walked briskly back up Vancouver to my undercover police car, trying to maintain the "command presence" that I'd been told was an integral part of being a competent police officer. If you acted weak or soft, you might get assaulted. If you acted strong and tough, you'd likely survive the night. The car was still intact when I arrived, no broken windows, and no Teddy Bears stolen.

This was a stark contrast to what had happened to my partner Danny Stohl when he worked vice with the same Teddy Bear car only a couple of years before. He had gone into Van's and an hour later when he came out, he discovered a busted out window and several missing Teddy Bears. He joked with me while telling me the story that "even Teddy Bears" weren't safe in the Albina ghetto.

I still had two more places to check before my shift was over, King's Tavern and the afterhours gambling joint located in a tiny corner house at 3836 North Vancouver. Both were just a few blocks apart and well-known spots for constant vice activity. Well aware how much alcohol I had consumed in-the-name-of-the-law, I got behind the wheel, started the car and carefully pulled away from the curb. I drove south on Vancouver and turned left at Fremont and left again onto NE Williams. King's Tavern was just ahead on Williams Avenue. I pulled up to the curb a half a block away and on the opposite side of the street so I could get a look at the front door which was propped open with a large rock painted bright white.

Having been inside when I was in uniform with my Coach Fred Brock, I knew better than to go in by myself in jeans and a jacket. The place was dangerous. With the front door open I could see the place was full of drunks, some of them bickering and squabbling. Cigarette smoke drifted out the door along with the sounds of Ray Charles yelling: "*I can't stop loving you!*" I could hear every word, the music was so loud.

People were going in and out, and some were drinking from cans of Old English 800 which they'd purchased inside. King's Tavern was a real dump, smelly and unclean; it was one of the worst taverns in Portland. "It was a typical night at Kings Tavern…" my report would read later that night. There had been many shootings at King's Tavern in the past, and knifings, and I wondered how many of the drunks inside had guns or were wanted on old warrants.

The house at 3836 North Vancouver Avenue was an after-hours club. We routinely watched the house to see what was going on. On a particular night that I was working vice, on my last stop of that night, I parked across the street and walked to the house. I had to sneak into the yard to peek in one of the ground floor windows, so I could see what was going on inside. I hated doing it. It felt cheap and sneaky, *and* dangerous.

Walking up to a window and looking inside made me feel like a degenerate. All I could see was the corner of a table, but it was enough. The old tattered beige pull-shade was down almost flush to the bottom of the window, but there was a tiny scrap of open space to peek through. I saw the table edge, and a Black man holding playing cards in his hand. It was not very sinister, I thought, but if they were gambling then they *were* breaking the law. The only legal gambling allowed in Oregon was parimutuel betting on horses and dogs. Portland had both and the state got its cut. Playing cards and drinking beer didn't seem like much of a crime to me and I *never* arrested anyone for gambling, even when I was a rookie patrolman and told I should.

By the time I made a few notes in my field notebook about King's Tavern and the after-hour's card game, it was quitting time. After I got in my car, I made a loop around Albina, down Vancouver to Russell and back up Williams to Killingsworth. I could see that the cars on the streets were thinning out. It seemed like the late night crowd were as high as they could get, as drunk as they could get, as rich as they could get, or as broke as they could get by four in the morning.

There were a few hangers on at the afterhour's clubs but they too would be heading home by daylight. It was transition time,

time for the night people to turn their domain over to the daytime working people and it was time for *me* to get something to eat.

There were three all night restaurants open in the area, the Burger Barn at Union and Shaver, Fuller's, which was an all night cafe on Union at NE Brazee, and Denny's on Grand Avenue in the Lloyd Center. I decided to go to the Burger Barn as it was the closest place and I was hungry for their excellent Chicken-in-a-Basket dinner. It was the kind of hungry you get from drinking all night and it made me feel ravenous. I couldn't wait to get at that chicken!

I parked a block away, as my Teddy Bear Ford was too conspicuous for that area and time of night, and briskly walked a block over, to the front door, carefully monitoring my slightly unsteady steps and at the same time making sure I was aware of my surroundings. I was a white man in the ghetto in the middle of the night. I was a cop, undercover, but still I had to be careful, because I could easily have become a target.

The Burger Barn was the best greasy burger joint around. They had great pork ribs made with their own special homemade barbecue sauce, breaded catfish, and homemade banana pudding, all of which I loved. They also made great cheeseburgers and the best crispy, greasy French Fries in town, perfect after a long night of drinking. The front of the restaurant opened directly onto the street. As I strolled up, I opened the door and went in, standing for a moment and looking for an open counter stool. There were ten stools, one which was always broken.

I took an empty stool close to the door and sat down wearily.

The waitress was a young, thin Black woman in her twenties, with a short afro dyed dark red. She wore dangling pearl earrings that swung back and forth when she moved and had a smooth bright complexion. She greeted me with a coffee pot in her hand and a friendly once over gaze. I was a familiar face but I was out of context. She wasn't quite sure she recognized me. The last time she'd seen me I was in uniform with my coach Fred Brock, and I could see the wheels turning in her mind, as she was trying to place me.

"What are ya havin' sir?" she asked with a smile.

Her pink frost lipstick was pearly white and it glittered, giving her mouth a jewel-like quality. It contrasted with her bright skin and set off the color of her golden brown eyes. I tried not to stare but this girl was pretty and she was hard not to look at.

"I'd like your Chicken-in-a-Basket. Make it with two thighs and some of your famous greasy fries."

"Famous, huh? Okay!"

"And gimme some of that banana pudding you guys make, with whip cream on top." She shrugged without answering and wrote down the order in her ticket book.

"What's your name?"

"I'm Sally, pleased to meet you, sir."

"Likewise."

"You want the coffee, too?" she asked, wiggling the pot at me as she held it in her hand. I smiled a yes and nodded my head, watching her as she turned to prepare my order and get a cup for me. Behind the counter was a grill for cooking hamburgers, a French Fryer and a single burner coffee pot. There were four or five other people at the counter, all lost in their hot coffee and cheeseburgers. I could tell by looking at their faces, they were as tired as I was. We all ignored each other, grateful for the quiet, and the sounds of the radio playing in the background.

By the time I finished my first cup of coffee, the chicken was in front of me. It was fried golden brown and looked perfect. I couldn't wait to dig in. The waitress stared at me for a moment as she carefully refilled my coffee. I think she was still trying to figure out where she had seen me before, but it hadn't clicked yet. The chicken was piping hot and when I bit into it some warm juice squirted a little dart back into the basket, landing on some French Fries. Of course it was delicious and crisp and tasted great as only food tastes to a hungry drunk, but it was also delicious because food at the Burger Barn was *always* delicious, even the standard cheeseburgers they made were perfect.

I stuffed the fries in my mouth and washed them down with gulps of now lukewarm coffee. I was hungrier than I realized. I hadn't eaten anything except bar peanuts since I'd had dinner at home, (meatloaf, mashed potatoes and green peas) before I went to work at 8:00 p.m. After finishing the chicken and fries, I pushed the spoon into the Banana pudding, scraping up the whipped cream and savoring every bite. It was sweet and good, and made with real bananas, blended in the pudding and layered on the bottom. In my drunken state, I randomly wondered why something sweet was always desirable after eating a savory meal. Everybody ate dessert after dinner—why was that?

I finished my late night meal and waited for the waitress to bring me the ticket for the food and coffee so I could pay her. After she sashayed over to the counter, I handed her a crisp ten dollar bill, and when she brought my change, laying it on the counter in front of me, she quietly asked: "You a cop aint-cha?" with a sideways smile. She leaned over the counter, wiping it clean with a bleached washrag. I didn't answer but just shrugged instead, and that seemed to pique her curiosity even more.

"You used to come in here a while back."

"Really? You sure you got the right guy?"

"Yep, I *never* forget a face!"

I smiled without answering, giving her direct eye contact, but left all the change as a generous tip and a reward for her finally figuring out I wasn't just another white late-night John grabbing a bite to eat before heading home to the Mrs. I felt a sense of smugness that I had confused her for awhile, but she was friendly and pretty and so I nodded again as I left and smiled appreciatively. She smiled back and I could tell if I'd stayed longer, she might even have flirted.

Stepping outside I paused for a minute trying to remember where I'd parked the police car. Remembering it was just a block away I fumbled for the keys in my pocket. I looked around me, checking my surroundings. I was still a white guy out late in the ghetto. I nudged the gun in my pocket. It was still there. By the time I drove downtown, parked the police car in the designated spot in the basement of Police Headquarters, and took the elevator to the second floor Vice office, my partner Danny Stohl was just finishing marking up his time card.

"Hey, Don, how was your night?"

"It was okay, not much goin' on."

"Yeah, same here."

"You get anything tonight?" I asked Danny.

"I wrote two jaywalking tickets to a couple guys coming out of that gay bar on Yamhill, and I busted an old hooker in the Old glory."

"The Old Glory sure is a dump. Be sure and take a shower when you get home. You don't know *what* you'll pick up in *that* place. Fleas? Ticks? Mice, maybe?"

"Yeah, it was real smelly tonight, some old coot puked in the corner."

"Did you know in the middle 1940s—somewhere in there—the Old Glory got in trouble for not servin' enough food?"

"Is that right?"

"Yeah, the Liquor Commission fined 'em for it. Told the owners they had to serve more food if they were gonna sell all that booze."

"So, what about you, Don? Any luck?"

"No arrests, just watching the heroin trade in Albina. You eat anything?"

"Yeah I grabbed a ham and cheese sandwich and a couple a

them egg rolls at the Sun Sang across the street. I think they got something goin' on in the back room over there, too. Maybe some kind of Chinese gambling, or something."

"There's *always* something goin' on in the back room of a Chinese joint!" I said with a chuckle.

"Got that right!" Danny responded.

"Have you seen the Lieutenant?"

"No but he left a note–said he'd see us tomorrow."

"He probably went home early," I said, waxing philosophical.

"Yeah probably. RHIP, ya know?"

"Yep, rank *does* have its privileges."

"See ya tomorrow, Don."

"Tomorrow old man, tomorrow."

We locked the office door behind us and shared a wave as we left the building going our separate ways, glad to be headed home where we would collapse into bed and get some needed rest, to get ready for the next difficult shift.

It was 5:30 by my watch when I unlocked my car, which was parked on Third Avenue. Daylight was just beginning to emerge through the dark Portland clouds and the car was covered in droplets of silvery morning dew. I unlocked the driver's door, and slipped behind the wheel. After fastening my seat belt, I turned on the engine, cranked up the defroster and turned on the windshield wipers to clear the windshield. I pressed the button that released two squirts of windshield washer fluid which helped the process along. It was a half hour drive from the police station downtown to my house on SE 77th and Duke Street in the suburbs.

Driving home in total silence always, (I never turned on the radio) gave me time to reflect on what I'd seen in a different district just a few miles away, which was in reality a different world altogether. It was a different economy, with a different mindset, and very different people. The Black community in Albina seemed to have so much joy and good humor in the way they related to each other and even to the white people they might be friends with. It was fun to listen to their "Yo Mama," jokes that you could almost forget there was also so much evil going on, from the drug dealing and prostitution to the rampant and heartbreaking domestic violence, which impacted women and children most.

The truest and most destructive evil of course was the heroin trade which destroyed so many lives. It was tolerated by the white power structure in Portland, and contributed to the overall misery of the Black community in Albina. The power players who made the rules about which crimes would be investigated and which crimes *wouldn't*, chose to look the other way. They chose not to see what they didn't want to see and pretend it wasn't really happening.

When I finally got home, I made my way into the house, tiptoed into my bedroom, undressed and slipped into bed beside my wife, trying not to exhale my fumes of alcohol breath on her. I felt like a cheater who had been out boozing and chasing women all night. I didn't *like* the way it felt. I didn't like working Vice. It felt wrong and bad. I didn't like the drinking. I didn't like *having* to drink, and I didn't like the lying, and pretending to be someone I wasn't.

I didn't know how long I could survive working Vice and without even consciously thinking about it, my mind began to wonder about some kind of transfer. *Any* transfer, just so I could feel good about myself again, and not like I was betraying the uniform I had sworn to honor and which I was dedicated to honor.

As I lay in bed, I closed my eyes and remembered Thelma dancing on top of the piano in her pasties, with her perfect body undulating to the music, her vacant eyes and her frozen, crazy smile. I wondered how long she would live, when she would die, whether she would *ever* be able to kick heroin. I thought about Thelma until I fell asleep, wondering how such a beautiful girl could be so doomed by everything and everyone around her.

The next few months working vice I would sit in the Cotton Club, in my usual spot by the stage, where I could see the door. I'd see the same faces walk in almost every night. This included Jaynolen Moody and Thelma, Buck Owens and Pam, Sherman Jackson and Henry Johnson, with various other women tagging along. I heard once that Mayor Terry Shrunk also showed up periodically at the Cotton Club, although I never once saw him there. He must have arrived after I left. During all this, Paul Knauls, allowed a youngster, a 17-year-old, light skinned Black teenager to play drums in his band and perform in his club. He looked so young as I recall. They called the boy Ronnie.

Years later, I learned his name was Ron Steen and he had been sitting in on jam sessions since he was 15. His parents must not have cared that he was a minor and could have been put in serious danger cavorting in a club meant for grown adults smoking and drinking liquor. Minors, of course, were *not* allowed on the premises, per Oregon Liquor Control Regulations during the seven years the Cotton Club was in operation from 1963-1970, when it finally closed its doors. But Oregon laws never prevented minors from being served at the Cotton Club.

My conclusion, during the time I worked Vice and regularly went to the Cotton Club to observe what was going on, was that Paul Knauls was either involved in or ignored the criminal activity going on within the Cotton Club, including allowing a teenager to play in the band until 2:30am. Knauls was surprisingly open about borrowing $50,000 from Mr. Way Lee to finance the club and has publicly discussed having done so.

This was the same Mr. Way Lee who was the top banana at the top of the heroin dealer flow chart in the PPB Vice office where I worked in 1963.

In fairness, to Mr. Paul Knauls, the 1960s was a time when no legitimate bank would loan money to a Black businessman. Enter the *Bank of Heroin* and Mr. Way Lee, who was happy to finance a Black owned nightclub *and* have an outlet for his heroin trade. Paul Knauls publicly boasted about paying off the $50,000 mortgage in three short years and even had a mortgage burning ceremony right on the stage of the club. It's easy to see that Knauls could not likely have paid off a debt of fifty thousand dollars so quickly just by selling whiskey and beer, alone and it's also easy to see why Knauls was proud the debt had been paid in full. He was full legal owner of the building and that was a rare thing in the Black community in Albina, to actually own property outright.

Knauls always managed to stay clean himself, being a non-smoker, a nondrinker and an ambitious, educated, and hard-working man. To this day I see Paul Knauls as a good man who may have done some risky things back in a time when Black people had to do the best they could with what they had. Knauls was known as a generous man who helped numerous people in the Black community, when they needed it most, loaning them money and helping out in other ways. Skirting the law was a necessity for many Black men in Portland, especially during the 1960s when good paying jobs were scarce for men of color, and the Portland political structure of policy makers didn't seem to care much about what happened to the Black population in the North End.

It became obvious to me, working as a patrolman and later on in Vice that as one person, I could do virtually nothing to stop the heroin business, which represented such a robust lifeblood to the economy. Heroin and prostitution was supported or ignored by Mayor Terry Shrunk, who himself enjoyed the drinks and the girls at the Cotton Club, who were generally Black and attractive. Captain Jim Purcell Junior kept two whorehouses going in Albina and his influence was a huge part of the problem. It seems that as long as heroin stayed in Albina and out of the white neighborhoods, on the west and SE side of town, heroin was okay with Terry Shrunk and Jim Purcell Junior. It didn't seem to matter how many young lives it took or how many families it devastated, cutting its wide swath of chaos and heartache.

****

My last night working Vice began as they all did, hanging around the house, after having dinner with my wife, and waiting for eight o'clock to roll around so I could leave for work. That night, I drove downtown, and crossed the Morrison Bridge, enjoying the fragrant Portland breeze. I got to the police station and found a place to park on Third Street, walked in the front door and up the marble steps, dressed in jeans and a plaid shirt and old denim jacket.

In the Vice office Lt. Jack Strudgeon greeted me with a cheerful hello and a twenty dollar bill in his hand for my nights drinking money. Strudgeon was a tall, well built man in his late forties. He had a crew cut and a full head of silver hair, a strong jaw and a stern attitude from having come up as a tough street cop in the 1940s. He looked like a tree trunk that could stop a train. Danny Stohl was already in the office reading the vice reports from all three Portland precincts to see if anything new had developed, or any new characters had come to town to cause trouble. His twenty dollar bill was placed on the desk in front of him. I watched as he absently tucked the bill into his shirt pocket, still reading the report, engrossed.

"Hey Don, looks like there's a new hooker workin' outa the Old Glory."

"A new one? I bet *she's* a gem. When did you find that out?"

"Just now, one of the district officers I talked to in the basement, just a few minutes ago."

"Maybe we can find her and put a health hold on her till Monday?"

"Sounds like a good place to start your shift, Danny, hop to it you two."

Danny smiled over at the Lieutenant and pointed at his own emerging belly with the butt of his snub nosed .38 barely showing behind his leather belt.

"I don't hop much anymore, boss. I'm lucky to be able to hump around."

"Oh come on, Danny, you're not even 40 yet!"

"But I *feel* 40, Strudgeon! A cop's life is a hard life, ya know?"

"You two are both kids! I'm 48! Get to work!"

The Lieutenant smiled and Danny and I laughed. On this light note I picked up the keys to the Teddy Bear Ford and tossed them to Danny.

"You drive, Danny. I drove last time."

"No problem."

"I'll probably be here at quitting time tonight," Strudgeon said glumly as he began to walk out the door.

"You don't have to wait up, Lt? We're gonna be gone a while," Danny said.

"I've got some paperwork to do and I might do some pushups."

"I can't remember the last time I did any pushups, boss."

"And it shows, Danny boy!"

"Well, thanks Lieutenant!"

We walked out the door and down the stairs to start our night working Vice. Danny felt slightly insulted by Strudgeon's comments and complained.

"Can you believe that guy? Is that all he does is workout and hang out with the girls at Bill's Gold Coin?"

"Who knows, and who cares? Let's get going."

"Where should we get to first?"

"Let's just ride. Cruise Broadway. See what's goin' on."

We drove up SW Broadway, the heart of busy downtown and back down 6th Avenue and made the loop a few more times. It reminded me of when I was a teenaged high school boy, out rapping the pipes of my car and looking for girls. People were out in the streets parking their cars, and going to dinner and the movies. Twinkling Marquees along Broadway showed the latest films, "Who Shot Liberty Valance," "State Fair" and "Music Man" were displayed prominently on the flashing marquees of the Liberty Theater, the Paramount and the majestic Broadway Theater.

We drove by Jolly Joan's restaurant and saw that it was packed with a few people waiting out front to get inside. We parked across the street from the Benson Hotel and just sat watching the line of taxis in front of the hotel with folks arriving and leaving. They looked like rich people, all well dressed and driving fancy cars, the ladies stepping out of the back seats slowly, displaying their stylishly covered legs in shiny nylon stockings, and wearing black high heeled pumps.

A rented Rolls Royce was parked in front loading partygoers in formal dresses and tuxedos. The vibe was happy. The vibe was good. After an hour of people watching and seeing nothing we wanted to get involved in, Danny cranked up the Ford and drove down to the tenderloin district, a mere four or five blocks away.

"I suppose we should check out the Old Glory first," said Danny glumly.

"God, do we have to go *there?*"

Danny drove around until we found a parking spot on Third Avenue across from the rundown Hamilton Hotel. We could already feel the vibe had changed in our new environs. The people on the streets were not well dressed and probably high or drunk or both. The flickering neon signs advertising cafes, bars and decrepit hotels were dingy looking; the sidewalks spotted with old gum, cigarette butts, candy wrappers and discarded chewing tobacco containers.

The rank odor of old urine drifted to our nostrils from some of the locked doorways to closed up businesses. We saw the occasional woman, walking alone, slumped over, defeated and sullen-faced. They were either on their way home from working as janitors in the office buildings, or loitering on the corners, looking for trouble in the form of someone who would buy them a drink, or take them home and give them booze in exchange for some human connection, whatever *that* turned out to be.

We locked the car and walked the two blocks to the Old Glory located at 118 SW Main Street. There was never a happy atmosphere in the tenderloin; it was always dark, forlorn and edgy. We walked aware of our surroundings and glanced over our shoulders. I wondered if the streetlights were deliberately less bright in this part of town. It seemed darker, less lit in places. We both unconsciously nudged our guns. We knew where we were.

We could see the Old Glory was crowded. I decided to stand outside and let Danny go in and see what he could see. When the door opened I could smell the alcohol fumes and see the cigarette smoke wafting towards the street, almost as if the place might be on fire. The place smelled bad, it had the toxic atmosphere of unclean bodies, unclean restrooms, and people who looked like they slept in a dumpster and never combed their hair, or bathed. It gave me the creeps looking into that hellhole, and Danny didn't stay long.

"Nothing in there I wanna be involved with!" Danny said, hurrying out the door and taking a deep breath of fresh air. "Besides, somebody puked in the corner and they haven't even cleaned it up!" Danny was indignant. "You sure it wasn't the puke from *last* time we were in there?" I asked, laughing at my own joke.

"Wouldn't be surprised!"

"Why do they even *have* a business license?" I asked, not expecting an answer. Danny shrugged, and stuffed his hands in his pockets, looking at the pavement as he walked beside me.

"Because the Mayor never comes here, that's why. Let's go see

Otto at the Lotus, instead," Danny said.

"Yeah, I guess we should go see Otto."

We walked west two blocks to SW Third Avenue and turned right leaving the rancid stench of the Old Glory behind us and still looking over our shoulders occasionally. Although we looked like two regular guys just walking down the street we didn't want anyone to mistake us for potential victims, we were cops, we were armed and we were *not* to be fucked with.

The Lotus bar and hotel was in front of us just a couple blocks away. As we walked by where our car was parked, we looked over to see if it was still intact. It was. In this part of the tenderloin cars were broken into all the time, and it was a concern that *our* car might be broken into. As we reached the Lotus we peeked in the front door to see how busy they were. The bar was busy with both men and women sitting, talking, smoking and swiveling on their stools, chatting it up, laughing, and having a good time.

Danny shut the main door and we walked across the room, to the other entrance, leading up the darkened stairs that led to the second floor. We trudged up the dark stairwell, the padding under the carpet cushioning every footfall. We were completely silent as we walked. The Desk Clerk occupied the first room which was number 9, on the right. Guests were checked in after signing the register and given their key. A room for rent by the day, the week, or in some cases by the hour was how the Lotus did business. Their policy invited all sorts of colorful, mixed-up characters. It was all up to Otto. Otto lived at the Lotus, working as Manager and Desk Clerk, registering guests and sometimes working all night. He was also the resident busybody, knew everyone and was a longtime reliable snitch of Danny's.

I hit the button which read "Push for Assistance," and heard a quiet bell ring. After a minute or so, Otto appeared from behind a partition where he slept, looking groggy and unkempt. Otto was squat and thick, and at barely five foot five he was barrel-chested with short thinning grey hair which he generally only had to comb with his fingers. He had three or four missing teeth but when he smiled it didn't seem too noticeable. Otto had been a merchant seaman for fifteen years and had seen most of the world by boat, shedding a few unfortunate women along the way, but that was when he was younger and more attractive. When Danny and I knew Otto, all he could attract were a few drowsy dust mites.

Otto arrived in Portland on a grain ship in the late 1940s, and decided to stay after looking over our sleepy port town. He found a room at the Lotus hotel, and ended up living there, keeping his apartment tidy, and sparsely furnished with an assortment of house plants that he tended to with the loyalty of a devoted pet owner. He was hired on, because he was good at resolving conflicts and keeping the peace with the hooker trade which frequented the old hotel. Otto kept a three foot section of heavy water pipe wrapped with black electrical tape hanging in plain sight on the wall behind him. He had drilled a hole through the back top-end, and slipped a length of green wool twine through it. The pipe hung on the wall and sent a very clear message. It would be used for only one thing—bashing heads.

The door to room 9 was a half door. The top half, made of heavy glass opened and the bottom wooden half stayed closed and acted as the platform where the guest register was located. Danny looked over the guest register and I peeked over his shoulder. "A lot of John and Jane Doe's on the register," he commented, running his thumb down the page. "All aliases," he added, "a whole town full of Jane Does. Alice Smith, this and Susan Jones, that. I wonder why that is?"

"Well, I don't care if the guests *don't* want to share their real name," said Otto. "It's none of my business anyway *who* they say they are." Otto ran his hands through his hair again and grinned broadly. "My real name ain't Otto either," he said, chuckling through his missing teeth. "My *real* name is Otto spelled backwards!"

It took me a second but I spit on myself from laughing so hard, leaning over, my hand on Danny's shoulder. It took Danny a moment to react, as he lifted his head for a minute to think, and then he chuckled after the joke made sense to him, too.

"You're easy, DuPay!" Danny said, laughing.

"Glad ya liked that one, kid," Otto said good naturedly.

"One of the district cops says there's a new girl workin' this area," said Danny, recovering from Otto's joke. "Know anything about her?" Otto ran his finger through his hair again, what there was of it, and then rubbed his chin with a questioning look on his face, boldly staring at Danny, who then fished a twenty dollar bill from his pants pocket and laid it on the counter on top of the guest register.

"Come on, Otto, tell me what ya know. We don't got all night." That settled that and Otto happily shared a wealth of information.

"Her name is Ophelia, you know, like from Shakespeare? She's from Seattle here looking for a change of scenery, or so she told me."

"From Seattle?" Danny asked.

"Yeah, but she's pushin' fifty and has a lot of miles on her, tall and thin, short hair, dark skin, great boobs, nice clothes and real pretty, kinda looks Ethiopian. Still passable, but can't charge what she used to when she was younger. Still she doesn't look fifty, but I saw her driver's license and know her birth date."

"Any new smack around," I asked.

"Nah, just what the girls bring with them from their home neighborhood, ya know the Black district? I guess they need it so's they can do what they need to do."

Finding out all we needed to know from Otto, Danny gave him a friendly bump on the shoulder with his fist. "Keep in touch Otto, if anything changes or if you learn something important," he said. We hustled down the dark cold stairwell, and into the night air. The unmarked car was right where we left it and after we got in, we listened to the radio for a few minutes, looking around, but nothing interesting was happening. We sat for a moment wondering what to do next. But there was always something to do and calls to answer. Danny and I were productive and always wanted to work.

Let's return now to how I met Kathryn, who at the time was LeRoy's girlfriend and the mother of one of his children. This was in the middle 1960s and an unmarried woman with an illegitimate child was not common. Women like this paid the price by being known as pariahs and by being rejected as indecent, but there was something decent and naive about Kathryn that I liked.

I wanted to remain working in Albina and St. Johns or as they said on the street, "NOPO" as in *North Portland*. Several months later, I was lucky enough to get transferred to North Precinct as a uniformed district cop, the precinct responsible for policing most of the entire troubled North End.

The politics had not changed, though. Terry Shrunk was still mayor and Jim Purcell Jr. was still the precinct Captain and still managing his whorehouses. And Albina was still a dangerous place to be. I needed a good young partner to work with and was lucky enough to be assigned to work with Ray Jones for the graveyard shift. Ray was my age and lived in Scappoose. North precinct was the precinct nearest to his home, which was the main reason he was working there. We made a good team. We wanted to make some needed changes in Portland and knew it would be a challenge, but we were gung-ho, determined and up to the task.

Our first night working together Ray and I decided to start by checking out Van's Olympic Room. We parked the car by the front door and walked in. By the expression on his face, I could tell LeRoy wasn't happy to see me. He seemed confused for a moment though, because I was again in uniform, having left the Vice Squad. He nodded politely, and then rolled his eyes, shaking his head, almost in disbelief.

Ray and I sat at the end of the bar near the door. I ordered a cup of coffee. LeRoy pointed at the half full coffee pot on the burner. The coffee looked like it had been on all day, inky black and distastefully potent. When the coffee was put in front of me, it smelled old and burnt. I asked for a little cream, which LeRoy provided. I poured about a shot glass full of cream into the burnt coffee. I sipped it. It tasted terrible. But I drank it, anyway. Not used to working all night long, I knew I needed the caffeine.

Late one night I was parked at North Vancouver and Fremont watching the cars leaving the parking lot at Van's at the 2:30 am closing time. By now I knew who the regulars were and what cars they drove. After the last of the late crowd left, only two cars remained—LeRoy's tan Cadillac and an old Chevrolet. The Chevy rolled off the lot and onto North Vancouver. It stopped at the light at Fremont before turning left and then left again onto NE Williams Avenue. I could see there was a young woman driving. To say the car was a *beater* would have been gracious.

After following the woman for a few blocks I could see the car was a rolling wreck. It squeaked and groaned like only an old car will. Her right rear tail light must have had a short in it because it would stay on until she hit a bump and then it went off. It would stay off until she hit another bump and then the light would come back on again.

The license plates were valid but there was no license plate light working. I had to see who the woman was and why she was out driving in the middle of the night. I turned on my overhead red flasher and pulled her over. She pulled into a side street right away and I got out and shined my flashlight into the car as I walked over. She was alone. I asked for her driver's license which she gave me from a purse next to her in the front seat. Her name was Kathryn, she told me. "What are you doing out so late, miss?" I asked. "Ya know, you have a tail light out? And what were you doing at Van's?"

"I know the light is out. I just haven't had a chance to get it fixed," she said timidly.

"It's just an equipment violation but your light keeps popping off and on," I followed up. I began writing her a ticket for her tail light. "Now, about what you were doing at Van's?" I could see the girl was pretty without shining my flashlight directly on her face. She smiled at me with an innocent yet impish smile and seemed almost embarrassed. Pursing her lips together before she spoke, her lips showed a soft pink lipstick. I could smell no alcohol on her breath but I could smell her perfume, something faint, and floral. She smelled good. Before answering she swished her black, shoulder length hair out of her eyes and began to speak, carefully choosing her words.

"LeRoy Clarke and I have a daughter together…" she said slowly, wistfully. "I have to go there to get support money for her. She's in diapers still and… needs stuff." I felt awkward hearing the reason she was out so late. She looked white, with perhaps some Indian heritage. She didn't seem like someone the flashy, hotshot Cadillac drivin' LeRoy would be interested in and I was curious to learn more about her. But I could hear the radio in my car crackling and knew I had to cut our time short, and get to another call.

"Get your tail light fixed, miss," I said. I thought better of saying what I wanted to say, which was: "LeRoy should get you a better car!" He drove a Cadillac and his old lady is driving a junker Chevy? My already low opinion of LeRoy sank even lower seeing the way he treated his girlfriend and the mother of his child.

Kathryn didn't seem like the heroin type, more of a granola girl, or a hippie. For the next two years until late1967, when I was promoted to detective, Ray Jones and I continued to police Albina and we gave it a lot of effort. We had some success with stopping underage drinking and serving drunks until they passed out. We were able to close the *Wishing Well* and *Patti's Perch* in St. Johns for seven days for these violations.

The *Red Sands* on Union and Shaver lost their liquor license permanently for continuous drunken brawls which often spilled out onto the streets. In time, the tavern owners figured out serving teenagers and drunks was a poor business model and the loss of income wasn't worth it.

The success we had with the liquor issues in the taverns and bars of Albina did not carry over to the heroin problem, as both were completely different forms of crime. Our success in that area was miniscule; the heroin trade was tricky, as it involved much more money, secrecy and international drug smuggling. We were aware of a Mexican heroin dealer named Bennie Villarreal working "the Avenue." His MO was a little different in that he was a walker. He didn't have a car or he didn't want to spend his money on one, because he was probably a longtime addict himself.

One night I got lucky. Ray and I were checking the crowd of drinkers inside King's Tavern. I spotted Bennie in the back near the restrooms and when he saw me he started moving away from me toward the men's room, his eyes on me the whole time. I quickly pushed my way through the crowd and into the restroom, and caught Bennie in a corner by the urinal. He had his back to me and was pretending to piss. But he also had something in his mouth, I could see the protrusion, and I just *knew* they were heroin balloons.

I rushed across the room, slammed him against the wall, caught him with both my hands around his throat and lifted him up off the floor. "Spit 'em out!" I ordered. When Benny refused I squeezed his throat until he couldn't swallow. "Spit 'em out or I'll strangle you!" I yelled at him, my face three inches from his. I could see some dirt in the corner of his eyes, his face was coated with a thin layer of dust and grime, the whites of his eyes were bloodshot and he was getting redder in the face. His breath smelled like a fresh can of anchovies and his teeth were rotten. He looked like he had slept behind a dumpster for a week. He was an addict, alright!

I cut off his wind, and he began to pass out. I watched his mouth open and his tongue pushed out eight little balloons of heroin packed in colors of red and yellow, just as he began to gasp for air. By then I had my hand over his mouth and easily grabbed the balloons and stuffed them in my pants pocket, wiping my hand off on my leg. I turned Bennie around and quickly hand-cuffed him. Now that he could breathe easier, he was cussing me out and trying to spit on me and threatening to kill me. "Let me loose and I'll cut yer throat!"

I bum rushed him out the restroom door, reefing up his arms when he tried to resist, and pushed him through the crowd to our police car at the curb in front of the tavern. Ray was in the passenger side writing in his notebook and a drunk black male was handcuffed in the back seat laughing like a crazy person, and drooling on himself. I pushed the still swearing Bennie in the back seat beside Ray's prisoner, where they eyed each other warily and pressed against their side of the car, trying to get as far away from each other as possible.

"Looks like we should call the wagon,"

"Yeah, let's call old 99."

As weeks turned into months I continued to see Kathryn leave Van's about once a week, with her old Chevrolet putt-putting along, and her tail light flickering on and off. I let it go for a while, but when it didn't get fixed after a few months, I stopped her again. "Hey lady," I said walking up to the car searching the interior with my flashlight, "yer tail light is still out and you *still* have no license plate light." She offered her driver's license. "Do you even *have* insurance?" I asked impatiently.

She pursed her lips, licking the dryness away before she spoke. "Well, LeRoy keeps saying he'll get insurance for me...but not yet, I guess..." Her voice trailed off and she looked up at me questioningly. Her hair seemed to keep falling in her eyes and she brushed it back with her left hand, and I couldn't help but notice she was not wearing a wedding ring. "Well, Kathryn," I said, looking at her name on the license, "you can't be driving around out here in the middle of the night with messed up taillights and no insurance. I'm writing you another ticket, but just for the missing license plate light this time."

"Is it going to be expensive?" she asked, gazing up at me.

"If you get the light fixed and show the receipt to the traffic judge he'll probably suspend any fine." I shined my light around the inside of her car just snooping around, but didn't notice anything unusual. "I *could* take you to jail, you know, for no insurance?"

"Oh please don't."

She began rummaging around in her tan leather purse, next to her on the seat and finally handed me a business card with the name of an insurance agent on it. "LeRoy said he's been talking to this guy about insurance, but..."

"OK," I replied, "but you gotta get this stuff taken care of... eventually." Kathryn continued looking at me and smiling hesitantly. "I know, and I will, I promise!" she said. "Can I go now officer, I have my baby at home with Mother?"

I didn't answer but just switched off my flashlight and turned away, motioning for her with my hand, to get going. I had to maintain a businesslike attitude while on the job, but there was no denying, I felt a little guilty for keeping her from her baby. And knowing that she was a struggling single mother with someone like LeRoy as the father to her child, she couldn't have had it easy.

I watched as the flickering tail light popped off and on as she drove away and wondered what was going on with her. Kathryn was a question mark, polite but hard to figure out, and my cop mind was beginning to find her interesting. Ray honked the horn. We had another call to take.

"What's up with her? asked Ray, "what were you guys talking about?"

"She says she's LeRoy's old lady."

"Do you think she's a hooker?" he asked

"Nah, she says they have a baby together, and she doesn't look the type. She's too clean looking, kinda whole wheat, with nuts and seeds, not all made up like a whore ya know? A hippie type, I'd say. Where's the call?"

"We hafta cover car 28 on a family beef over on North Rodney. We've been there before and the old man is a mean drunk."

"Let's go."

Kathryn continued visiting LeRoy weekly leaving Van's at closing time. And I continued to pull her over every so often, usually about once a month, as she never did repair that taillight or get her license plate light hooked up, either. But I stopped writing her equipment violation tickets because she seemed genuine and never got angry at me for stopping her. Kathryn was always polite and politeness goes a *long way* with a tired hungry cop in the middle of the night.

But it was more than that. I didn't want to add to her financial burden or the struggles in her life. Her story was always the same, and it was similar to so many other women living in the Albina ghetto. She was trying to get money from LeRoy and get home to her baby. She seemed harried by her existence, trying to keep it together for her daughter.

After a year or so, I admit I stopped Kathryn several more times just to talk with her. It could get lonely on a slow night and she was always nice. Perhaps I was even attracted to her, I don't know. She was always so pleasant and she smelled good. She wasn't like the other denizens who haunted Albina after dark. She was clean and decent and seemed kind, maybe that's why LeRoy liked her?

I remember one of the first times I pulled her over just to talk, I told her: "You're not in any trouble and I'm not gonna ticket you. I just figured you wouldn't mind talkin' to me for a minute or two. It's pretty slow out tonight. How've you been and how's your old man treating you?" When Kathryn realized I just wanted to talk she smiled and relaxed and told me more of her story. From then on, I'd pull alongside her on the road, or sometimes motion for her to pull over but she knew I just wanted to visit.

It was always late at night and she never seemed to mind. She'd smile her Mona Lisa smile at me and we'd talk for ten or fifteen minutes about life, current events, what we had for dinner, or how expensive rent was getting in Portland. She seemed flattered that I cared enough to chat with her, without putting on the make or trying to hook up with her later.

Then I'd watch her drive off, her tail light flickering as she hit the bumps in the road and more often than not, I just shook my head feeling sorry for her. Kathryn seemed as decent as the criminals on the street seemed corrupt. She was just one of the odd people who crossed my path in the middle of the night in the ghetto that was The North End.

✴✴✴✴

Jaynolen Moody continued to drop off Thelma at Van's for her night's work shift. I noticed she was not dancing as often on the piano top. I would see her sitting at a back table where she could watch the front door for possible johns. She would sip from a tall glass of coke and something, fiddle with her nails, check her makeup in her little compact mirror and smooth down her long black wig, training the loose curls with her fingertips.

Thelma had lost weight, though. Her once voluptuous boobs were sagging now. She was not skinny yet but she was getting there. Her lifestyle of alcohol, heroin and the stress of prostitution was taking its toll. She was property, chattel. She was a possession. She was expendable. And when she was worn out and no longer of economic value, Moody would find a younger girl to replace her. Pimps like him were predictable in how they treated the girls in their stables.

In September of 1967 my tenure as a street cop in Albina and North Portland came to an end when I was promoted to detective. After being immersed in the problems of Albina for six years I had also become a victim, a victim of compassion fatigue. Seeing the same problems of alcohol and drugs and their aftermath had more than taken its toll. I was looking forward to a new job and a new challenge. It was time to pass the torch.

But retrospectively Thelma Moody did not die from heroin. She died from lead poisoning so to speak. On February 26, 1972 Thelma Zena Moody was shot and killed by Myra Moody, whose real name was actually Margaret Parker. At the time of the shooting Thelma was 29, and Myra was 26. They had gotten into an argument over the ownership of a cheap $10 dollar wig. A total "ghetto" happening.

Thelma pulled a knife on Myra and Myra happened to be armed that night. The knife flashed and the gun fired and Thelma lay mortally wounded on the dance floor of Van's Olympic Room, dying sometime later at Emmanuel Hospital. Margaret Parker received five years probation and a $500 fine. Thelma had made many mistakes in her fast life adventures but she failed ghetto rule 101.

Never bring a knife to a gunfight.

Northeast Portland, Oregon, 1980

Kathryn and I lay together on her bed fully dressed with a bag of weed between us, a lighter and an ashtray. We were each sipping beer from clear bottles of cold Miller's High Life. It was her favorite beer and I was happy to share it with her. We were rolling joints from some loose weed in a shoe box lid, getting high, enjoying each other's company and talking, bemusedly, about how our lives had come together after so many years of bumping into each other back when she was LeRoy's old lady and I was a fresh faced naive cop.

Her daughter was a teenager and so it had been quite a few years since we first encountered each other in the middle of the night in old Albina when I was a street cop and she had certainly been a person to take notice of.

Kathryn took a hit on the joint which I lit for her and then impishly blew the smoke in my face. "Whatcha doin' out here so late?" she asked, mocking what I used to say when I would stop her car for a tail light problem.

"Yeah, Kathryn, what *were* you doing out so late all those times?"

Kathryn continued the game. "Well, officer," she smirked, "I'm just getting money from LeRoy, and…and I have a baby at home." She laughed and it lit up her face, soft in the dim light of the bedroom, with the marijuana smoke drifting around our faces. The laugh lines were soft around her large brown eyes.

"You are enjoying this too much!" I said, gently poking her arm with my forefinger. "I admit you had me completely fooled. I thought you were just a nice girl in a bad situation and you made me feel *sorry* for you." She laughed again, genuinely happy to be with me, I could tell.

"But you were so innocent and young officer DuPay," she said, "and I *knew* you were just doing your job... and... after the first few times you stopped me, I knew I had you fooled." She giggled gloating to herself on how successful she had been at fooling me. "It was your junker car that threw me off, besides that it was your beautiful smile and that sweet smelling perfume."

"Plumaria!" she said, "and it's still my favorite perfume. It's from Hawaii." She pointed to her dresser and I saw all the perfume bottles and lotion lined up neat and orderly. "I still have some, although I don't wear it as often anymore."

"Well, it *was* really nice."

"Actually the Junker car was *my* idea."

"Why?"

"The truth is I was selling pot for LeRoy. He would give me the weed and I would sell it and keep most of the money. It was his way of taking care of us I guess."

"Wow!" I said. "I really was green. I'm embarrassed I was so easily fooled."

"Don't worry about it Don, you were so young."

"Yeah, I sure was, but so were you."

"Well, yeah, but…"

"But what?"

"Well, everyone of the players on the Avenue was driving a fancy shiny car, a Cadillac or a Duece and a Quarter. I figured a rattle trap car was the best car for haulin' pot—and it worked. The car looked like it belonged in the ghetto and no one ever bothered me driving it, no one but nosy you, that is."

"Yeah, the good old days, I guess."

I was quiet for a moment, relighting the joint and sipping on my beer. I was both annoyed and amused that this woman had so easily led me astray, when I thought I was a pretty sharp street cop. I could see Kathryn was reading my mind.

"Don't feel bad," she said, "LeRoy would tell me you were a pain in the ass district cop, always coming around, but he always knew where he stood with you. He didn't hate you or anything."

"You didn't look like the kinda gal LeRoy would be interested in," I mused mostly to myself."

"That was the secret I think," she replied. "Shabra and I were the decent quiet normal part of his life, the part he kept separate from the heroin business."

"I never thought of that but it makes sense now that you mention it. He was leading sorta… a double life. Full time bad guy, part time dad and provider."

"I was never involved in the heroin part because I knew it was a road to nowhere," she said, attaching a bobby pin to the remainder of the joint as a crutch before taking a final hit. "But weed is ok, never hurt anybody," she said, slowly blowing the smoke through her nose. "Shouda never been against the law anyway. Besides, I didn't care. There's enough Indian in me to wanna stick it to the white man and so what, ya know? I mean look at you, now."

"Yeah, I know."

"When did you start smoking it?"

"Oh, about three years after I became a detective, 1970, around there. I was 34."

After drinking three Miller beers and smoking two joints with Kathryn, I began to get sleepy. She found a soft pillow and lifted up my head, placed it under me, snuggling it into my neck, and then covered me with a satin and velvet "crazy quilt" her mother had made years ago, and I soon fell asleep.

****

Kathryn lived in a 1930s wood frame two-story house with a full basement. LeRoy had helped her buy it when Shabra was little. It was in Albina on North Borthwick at the corner of North Jessup, and still a good family neighborhood. The house had a small front yard with a lawn and the back of the house was located directly adjacent to an alley. It was originally painted light grey, but the paint had faded and looked dirty white.

Still, it was a good house with a wooden front porch that sloped from age and neglect slightly toward the four stairs leading up from the walkway. The front door was dark stained wood with fogged glass which allowed a little light into the front entryway. The kitchen was large and airy with dated linoleum of blue, gold and grey diamond patterns. Adjacent to the kitchen was a breakfast nook which seated four around a Formica table with windows looking out onto the back area of the alley.

I was often invited to dinner by Kathryn and one evening she was fixing mashed potatoes, corn on the cob and hot links. "You like hot links, doncha?" she asked. I had never eaten a hot link before but they looked like sausages to me as she dropped them into the boiling water.

"Sure," I replied confidently.

"How many do you want?" she asked

I looked at the package again. "Two," I said. They looked really good and I was hungry. With dinner prepared, we sat at the table directly across from each other and she put my plate in front of me first and then served herself. With a serrated table knife she cut off a big bite of the sausage and popped it in her mouth, chewing slowly and deliberately. I did the same; smiling and watching her eat her hot links.

But it wasn't the same. It was like biting into a bottle of Tabasco Sauce. I immediately regretted taking such a big bite and was forced to spit some out of it into my hand, in self defense. My mouth was on fire. Kathryn saw my dilemma and rushed to the sink to get me a big glass of cold water. I chugged about half of it down in one gulp.

"I thought you said you knew what they were?" she said, holding back a chuckle and enjoying my obvious discomfort.

"I thought it was just a sausage!" I gingerly took another small bite.

"Well, yes and no, but not exactly."

We settled into some easy conversation about nothing in particular when I smelled an aromatic smoke. I turned to see Kathryn's mother Rosalie standing at the top of the basement stairs, the door open, with Rosalie standing just behind the threshold. She was holding a smudge stick waving it around over her head. She nodded at me in acknowledgement but didn't say a word. She walked over to the stove and helped herself to a hot link spearing it with a fork. I watched in amazement as she popped half of it in her mouth before returning with the rest still speared on her fork, down to her basement apartment.

"Mom smudges every day," explained Kathryn. "She gets into all the corners because that's where bad spirits gather. In the corners ya know."

"In the corners?"

"You know why Indian teepees are round don't you?"

"I have no idea," I admitted, smiling.

"Teepees are round so no bad spirits can gather, and that's because there are *no* corners," she explained.

"Interesting. I never knew that."

"Well, now ya do!"

As I was eating the mashed potatoes and corn on the cob, I noticed behind Kathryn, on the wall, was a framed eight by eleven of LeRoy as a much younger man in his middle twenties. His hair was jet black, straightened and styled in a pompadour on top of his head and he sported a small neatly trimmed mustache. He was wearing a tan sport coat with a lighter tan sateen dress shirt. He was smiling and looked happy, and I could tell he was half or at least one third white.

Kathryn noticed me looking at the photograph and chuckled. "Nice lookin' guy," I offered in a friendly detached sort of way. "Yeah, he didn't look worried in that photo," she said.

"Worried is how I remember him behind the bar at Van's. His brow was always wrinkled up like he was concerned about something."

"And he was. He had the weight of the world on his shoulders most days."

"You know, Kathryn, in the six years I worked Albina, and all the times I saw him, or had to speak to LeRoy, he never actually *spoke* to me. He'd just nod his head or kinda grunt an affirmation, but I never heard his voice. Isn't that odd? What a strange guy he was."

Kathryn nodded her head towards the photo. "He was the most beautiful man I'd ever *seen!*" she blurted out. "He was smooth, ya know, satiny gorgeous skin, kinda pale. He knocked my socks off. And the rest of my clothes, too..." her voice trailed off in remembrance. "We had fun," she said, looking over her shoulder at the picture and shrugging. "He had money then, too, and didn't mind spending it."

"I remember he always looked nice, always had such nice clothes, always tan colored, beige or light brown, nothing bright or flashy.

"Yep, Don, that sounds like LeRoy. He liked things that were elegant, not stupid looking."

"That's now I remember him, too"

"You remember his Cadillac was tan?"

"That's right, I remember that, now you mention it."

"Then I got pregnant and things changed. We couldn't play anymore and there was no way I was gonna be in the heroin business *with* him. So, it worked out that I'd sell pot and we would work on gettin' a house together. That's how I first ran afoul of *you* runnin' around in the middle of the night, when I was getting money and weed from LeRoy."

"You sure had me fooled, Kathryn."

"Like, I said Don, you were so young and I knew you wanted to save the world from bad guys. You had stars in your eyes, then."

She stopped talking and her eyes clouded up, tears suddenly began rolling down her cheeks. The fork in her hand wavered and lowered, settling into the steaming pile of mashed potatoes, providing a path for a small pool of melted butter to drip onto the tablecloth, which she didn't seem to notice, and I didn't mention. Her head dropped and I saw tears fall onto the faded blue of her jeans.

"He didn't deserve to die that way! Shot to death by them cops!

And for what?!"

The energy of her explosive emotion hit me and I felt it reverberate on my face and in my hair, almost like a gust of wind. Having lost a few people in my own life, including my Black girlfriend who was murdered, I felt terrible for Kathryn, and reached across the table to hold her hand and comfort her. Of course, I already knew what happened to LeRoy. That he'd been shot to death in a shootout with the Swat Team inside of Van's in the summer of 1977 during a hostage situation was well known in the city.

There was a pile of paper table napkins on the table and I offered her one. She dabbed at her tears before continuing and took a deep breath, trying to calm herself. "You know Don, LeRoy was in the heroin business with Charlie Hill for years."

"You mean Sergeant Charlie Hill, the Narc Sergeant?" I asked, stunned. "Are you saying it was… *that* Charlie Hill?!"

"Yeah, *that* Charlie Hill. He sure was dirty, but he kept it all hidden."

"No wonder LeRoy always had a scowl on his face! That poor bastard got messed up with Hill! Why am I not surprised?!"

The truth is that I was stunned... but somehow also not surprised. After thinking about this revelation for a few minutes, I became disgusted and then I got angry. I wadded up a paper napkin and threw it on the floor. "That bastard!" I spat quietly. "I spent alotta time as the district cop tryin' to keep a handle on the smack business. I knew what LeRoy was doin' but I didn't know his partner was a damn cop! I feel... I feel fuckin' betrayed!"

"Betrayed?"

"I know it was a long time ago, but LeRoy was a known entity to me, but Hill?—that fuckin' snake in the grass! God damn him! Gettin' kids hooked?"

"Yeah," Kathryn answered, shrugging her shoulders.

"No wonder he always looked like a nervous wreck!"

"LeRoy was constantly worried something would go wrong—and it did."

"What was the deal, what happened?"

"I don't know all the details. We weren't that close in the last couple of years because he married…you know, that *other* woman?"

"Yeah, I think I remember her."

Kathryn put down the paper napkin and took another tentative bite of her hot link. She chewed and swallowed it with a sip of Cherry Kool Aid before speaking again. "I heard in a roundabout way that LeRoy and Hill had a falling out. Something went bad on one of the big heroin deals, some of it went missing, and I heard LeRoy was gonna have to go to prison, because Hill sure as hell wouldn't take the rap."

"That bastard…" I said again under my breath. "Sounds like they got busted, maybe the narcs or the feds got word, and Hill was gonna make LeRoy take the fall to save his own ass. All Hill would have to do was tell the narcs it was LeRoy's deal, and he had nothin' to do with it. And they'd believe him, too, cause he was a cop!"

"That's what I thought," Katheryn answered, sniffling and reaching for another napkin.

"Where was it all coming from?" I asked. "I always heard it was the Chinese. At least that's what I heard in the dicks."

"It *was* the Chinese," she answered. "It *always* came from the Chinese. You know that, Don!"

"Yeah, I know. Good old Way Lee."

"That's right. Way Lee. And I knew LeRoy was not gonna go to prison for Hill!" she continued. "I heard through the grapevine LeRoy was gonna set him up and ambush him when he showed up at Van's for the meet-up," she continued.

"And that's exactly what happened!" I interrupted. "I remember reading the Oregonian article on it. When Hill showed up, LeRoy blasted him with a 12 gauge and a .38 pistol. Hill wasn't killed but the cops, after they rescued Hill, opened up on him and LeRoy was blown away. He was hidin' in the dark. Stripped down to nothing but his black skin. Hiding in the dark."

"That's how it happened. Did you ever read what Hill said in that one article?"

"Which one?"

"In the Oregonian. They wrote two or three on that day. Anyway, he was quoted as saying, "I lost a friend today." Or something like that. I remember thinking, *why* would a cop say that?

Everyone knew LeRoy was a drug dealer, so why say that? It shows how crooked Hill was. So, one of his friends is a drug dealer? And *he's* a clean as a whistle, cop? Okaay!"

"He was no clean as a whistle, cop. He was dirty."

Kathryn broke out sobbing again, through her tears: "*He didn't have to die that way!*"she gasped weakly. There were no words I could conjure to take away the pain, so I got up and walked behind her and put my arms around her and held her for a moment. She looked up at me, embarrassed but grateful and returned my embrace and we continued with our dinner, changing the subject and talking about other things.

****

Kathryn and I remained friends, enjoying and always marveling at the oddity of our relationship and the statistical improbability of it all—ex-cop and ex-pot dealer who strangely became close friends in what seemed like another lifetime for both of us. And though we *were* attracted to each other, we never *did* have sex. I wanted her, and I believe she would have been receptive, but over time and without ever actually speaking on it, I think we both silently and tacitly decided sex would complicate an already unique relationship.

So we didn't go there. We respected each other enough and valued our friendship enough to protect it and keep it simple. In time my work at the Benson Hotel became more demanding, and we slowly just stopped meeting for coffee and dinner. Eventually we simply lost track of each other, but Kathryn will always remain someone precious to me, and someone I will *never* forget.

About the Author

Don DuPay was born in Wenatchee, Washington where he spent most of his childhood, later moving to rural Montana for a short time living on his parents farm. He settled in Portland, Oregon permanently in 1947 at the age of eleven. DuPay graduated from Grant High School in 1954 and later studied for 2 years at Lewis and Clark College. He went on to spend 3 years  active service duty in the US Navy performing top-secret radio surveillance on the Baltic Sea, during the Cold War. He rose to the rank of Cryptographic Technician T-branch E-6. From there, DuPay joined the Portland Police Bureau in 1961. In 1967, at the age of 31 he rose to the rank of detective and was later promoted to homicide detective. DuPay worked for PPB until 1978 when he resigned for documented medical reasons. He became the director of security for the Benson Hotel for several years in the 1980s, and was instrumental in changing hotel safety policies that would ensure better safety for customers and manage fire code violations. Later DuPay volunteered as co-host of a cable access television program called Cannabis Common Sense, with host Paul Stanford. In 2017, DuPay graduated from Portland State University. He was honored in the commencement program for being "the oldest" graduate of that year. DuPay resides in Portland with his 4th wife, author, poet and editor, Theresa Griffin Kennedy. The Tainted Rose: Stories from a Portland Detective, is his third book.

About the Illustrator

Truxton Meadows grew up in Yamhill, Oregon during the 1970s and 1980s, graduating from Yamhill Carlton High School. He studied at Palomar College, in San Marcos, California and is a Marine veteran, former Battalion S-1 from 1985 to 1988. He works as an artist and graphic designer with 23 years design & publishing experience. He sketches, paints, does illustration and experiments with mixed media, as well as pursuing photography. He is regularly adding to his Truxton Art & Illustration portfolio. His charming illustrations were used with permission in this book by author Don DuPay. Meadows currently lives and works in Estacada Oregon and is busy at work writing a series of introductory "zines" of lesser known American history for a new generation.

About the Editor

Theresa Griffin Kennedy was born in Baker, Oregon and has lived in Portland, Oregon since she was eight-months-old. She is a writer of creative nonfiction, poetry, literary fiction in the genre of domestic noir, and crime history. She works as a freelance editor and is the publisher and editor of *Oregon Greystone Press*.
In 2013 Kennedy completed a masters degree in *Adult Education, Leadership and Policy*, and in 2014, a masters certificate in *Teaching Adult Learners*. Kennedy is an advocate for prison reform through education, literacy and creative writing. She has been published in literary reviews, magazines, newspapers, several anthologies and in online news sources. Kennedy is the author of six books, including *Blue Reverie in Smoke: Collected Poems 2001-2016*, *Burnside Field Lizard and Selected Stories*, *Talionic Night in Portland: A Love Story*, *Beyond Where the Buses Run: Stories*, and *The Lost Restaurants of Portland, Oregon*. Kennedy is hard at work on her second novel, *The Garbageman of Thurman Street*. She is a native of Portland, Oregon, and is married to Don DuPay, a writer, author, and a retired homicide detective who worked with PPB from 1961-1978.